Advance Praise for
I Speak for Myself: American Women on Being Muslim

The women in *I Speak for Myself* are part of a new generation of peace-builders. By telling their stories they offer us new perspectives that are vital to the peace building process, and through their honesty and courage they are making a lasting contribution to the search for cross-cultural understanding. Maria Ebrahimji and Zahra Suratwala's book joins the mission for global tolerance; it is truly a step in the right direction. —HER MAJESTY QUEEN NOOR

A central part of combating intolerance between people is listening to each others' stories. In *I Speak for Myself*, 40 American Muslim women tell us their stories—stories of their faith, their families, their values, and their traditions. They are wonderfully human and widely diverse, both informative and inspiring. As in all of our faith traditions, the growing role of women will be crucial in shaping the future of Islam. This is a very important contribution to the growing interfaith dialogue in this country; I commend it to you."
—JIM WALLIS, FOUNDER AND CEO OF SOJOURNERS AND
AUTHOR OF *REDISCOVERING VALUES*

This book is a window into how Islam is lived in America by some of its most dynamic, creative, and inspiring leaders. The voices here are clear and compelling, compassionate and courageous. This is Big Tent Citizen Islam at its best—a community welcoming of its own internal diversity, and making important contributions to the broader society.
—EBOO PATEL, FOUNDER AND PRESIDENT INTERFAITH YOUTH CORE

I Speak for Myself showcases a part of our country's story we seldom hear. The book provides a window into the extraordinary lives of Muslim American Women--dynamic, diverse, and finally demystified. Ebrahimji and Suratwala inspire the reader and help fill a missing piece in the rich tapestry we call America.
—DALIA MOGAHED, DIRECTOR, GALLUP CENTER FOR MUSLIM STUDIES

As the dialogue on faith and spirituality progresses, women should not be overlooked. *I Speak for Myself* demonstrates that American Muslim women have a story and, more importantly, a unique voice in which to tell it. In an era where women's empowerment is essential, these are women who have the ability, through their stories and their work, to empower women all over the world to truly speak for themselves.

—MUHAMMAD YUNUS, NOBEL PEACE PRIZE WINNER & FOUNDER, GRAMEEN BANK

I Speak for Myself is a must read for anyone curious to understand Islam from a woman's and an American Muslim's perspective. This is the work of bridge makers; women who understand that their voices and their truths are one of the most solid, real, and powerful ways to promote understanding and peace between people of various faiths. Ebrahimji and Suratwala do a superb job in bringing these women's voices out with beauty, intimacy, and integrity. *I Speak for Myself* is the story of every woman embodied in voices of today's American Muslim woman.

—ZAINAB SALBI, FOUNDER, WOMEN FOR WOMEN INTERNATIONAL

Empowering girls through education does not stop in the schoolroom; a book like this can be just as influential in widening a young girl's view of the world and of her own potential within it. This collection of essays edited by Maria Ebrahimji and Zahra Suratwala is empowering and inspiring, and a vital part of any education.

—GREG MORTENSON, AUTHOR, *THREE CUPS OF TEA*

I Speak for Myself is a beautiful compilation of stories reflecting the diversity in Islam and the common values that exist among us all. These are the voices of mothers, daughters, sisters and neighbors we can all identify with representing an honest effort to allow American-born Muslim women to change the narrative of American Islam—in their own words.

—DEEPAK CHOPRA, AUTHOR, *THE SOUL OF LEADERSHIP*

Nothing succeeds like success. *I Speak for Myself* is a powerful reminder that the American dream transcends race, gender, and creed. Here is a collection by individuals who are successful in every conceivable way: as women, as Muslims, as individuals, as leaders, as role models—as Americans. Each of them reminds us that personal inspiration is the strongest kind. Each story is so rich that generalizations and stereotypes become impossible. These women are the real Americans.

—PARAG KHANNA, AUTHOR, *THE SECOND WORLD;*
FELLOW, NEW AMERICA FOUNDATION

This unique compilation of Muslim voices gives a window into a culture in transition and growth. Bravo to these women for sharing themselves with us.

—SOLEDAD O'BRIEN, CNN ANCHOR AND SPECIAL CORRESPONDENT

Too rarely are Muslim women's voices heard. *I Speak for Myself* is an extraordinary collection of essays that lets Muslim American women speak for themselves. It is refreshing, inspirational, honest, and ultimately, an indispensable guide. I must congratulate the editors for their important contribution.

—PROFESSOR AKBAR AHMED, AMERICAN UNIVERSITY

I Speak for Myself is exactly the kind of book we so desperately need right now in America. We don't need more books on Islam and what Muslims believe; we need books on Muslims and how they are trying to live in America just like the rest of us. Americans have had the perception that Muslims are not as "American" as the rest of us. That simply isn't true. I loved reading the story of a woman wrestling with her identity in her faith and some of the issues just like the rest of us non-Muslims as we wrestle with issues of our faith. Muslims do not want to "take over" America; they are searching for a place to see dreams come true. Only when we can see them as Americans wanting to experience the same dreams as everyone else will we be able to get along. I'll be promoting and passing out this book.

—PASTOR BOB ROBERTS, NORTHWOOD CHURCH, KELLER, TX,
AND FOUNDER OF THE GLOBAL FAITH FORUM

I Speak for Myself is a collection of Muslim American women's stories about their relationships with both non-Muslims and fellow Muslims, their search for their own identities, and how faith shapes their lives. The book gives valuable perspectives and insight into an often little understood segment of America's changing society.

—ROXANA SABERI, IRANIAN-AMERICAN JOURNALIST AND AUTHOR OF
BETWEEN TWO WORLDS: MY LIFE AND CAPTIVITY IN IRAN

Maria Ebrahimji and Zahra Suratwala have undertaken a fantastic and truly inspiring project that gives voice to those that have yet to be heard: Muslim American women. I have great respect for their efforts on this wonderful and very essential initiative, *I Speak For Myself*, and am sure that those that read it will appreciate its uniqueness and relevance. My hope is that these refreshing voices are heard and help to provide a deeper insight into the diversity of expression and perspectives.

—DEEYAH, MUSIC PRODUCER, COMPOSER, AND ACTIVIST

I Speak for Myself is a testimony to our shared values and common faith: stories that illustrate one single destiny which strengthen our bonds of concern, compassion and caring for each other.

—RABBI MARC SCHNEIER AND RUSSELL SIMMONS, PRESIDENT AND CHAIRMAN,
RESPECTIVELY, OF THE FOUNDATION FOR ETHNIC UNDERSTANDING

I Speak for Myself

A Note about the *I Speak for Myself* series:

I Speak for Myself is an inclusive platform through which people can make themselves heard and where everyone's voice has a place. ISFM's mission focuses on delivering one core product, a "narrative collection," that is mindset-alerting, inspiring, relatable, and teachable.

We aim to deliver interfaith, intercultural titles that are narrow in scope but rich in diversity. To learn more about the series, join the conversation, and even create an *I Speak for Myself* book of your own, please be sure to check out our website: www.ISpeakforMyself.com

ZAHRA T. SURATWALA AND MARIA M. EBRAHIMJI
I Speak for Myself co-founders

BOOKS IN THE SERIES

Volume 1: *I Speak for Myself: American Women on Being Muslim*

Forthcoming titles will cover the following subjects:

Volume 2: *American Men on Being Muslim*
Volume 3: *Voices from the Arab Spring Movement*

I Speak for Myself

American Women on Being Muslim

Co-Editors Maria M. Ebrahimji and Zahra T. Suratwala

WHITE CLOUD PRESS
ASHLAND, OREGON

Design by Confluence Book Services

First edition: 2011

Printed in the United States of America

2016 2015 2014 2013 2012   5 4 3 2

Library of Congress Cataloging-in-Publication Data

I speak for myself : American women on being Muslim / co-editors:
Maria M. Ebrahimji and Zahra T. Suratwala.
p. cm.
ISBN 978-1-935952-00-8
1. Muslim women--United States. 2. Muslim women--Religious life-
-United States. 3. Women in Islam--United States. I. Ebrahimji, Maria
M. II. Suratwala, Zahra T.
BP67.A1I2 2011
297.082'0973--dc22
2011008790

To our family and friends near and far: you have empowered us to lift our voices. Without you, we would not be who we are today. We love you and thank you for your support.

Table of Contents

Note on Transcriptions

In transcribing Arabic, Persian, Urdu and other foreign words and names, we have chosen not to use diacritical marks and the like as found in scholarly literature. On first usage, a foreign word will be italicized and its definition given in the Glossary at the back of the book.

Introduction

We are women. Muslim. American. Women. We share one of many American faiths—a faith that is the fastest growing in the world, with more than 1.5 billion followers. We are committed to our faith as much as we are bound to our national identity. We speak for ourselves.

In the early stages of contemplating this collection of essays, we wondered what we would ask our contributors to write about. Would we give them a concrete theme and ask them to relate their essays to it? If we left the theme open, would several of the essays end up revolving around the same issues anyway? Would we receive essays that were honest, introspective, and affirming? We weren't sure how best to approach this process.

One thing we were certain of is this book is a necessary contribution to the existing forum of ideas and voices that are informing Americans and other citizens of the world about our existence. Other books about Muslim women were written from someone else's perspective. Or they weren't about Muslim *American* women. Or they weren't completely personal narrative. We wanted to combine all of these aspects into one book: first-person narratives written by women who were born and raised in America and have been negotiating the dichotomy between Islamic and Western values since birth.

Most of our colleagues and sisters in this book have never outwardly expressed their personal stories or views, much less had them published. For this reason alone, this project is unique—a refreshing opening into our lives, our minds, and our hearts. Those of us who contributed to this book didn't do so to respond to stereotypes, pontificate about a post-9/11 world, or emphasize how "normal" or "advanced" or "educated" we all are. We don't question our allegiances to our country or our faith. We value both.

The contributors to this book come from every corner of our community: environmentalist, mother, blogger, academic, feminist, spiritualist, conservative, fashionista, coach, lecturer, engineer, perpetual student, truth-seeker, sister-in-humanity, activist, advocate, writer, teacher, artist, lawyer, journalist, anthropologist, aid worker, consultant, and Facebook friend.

Through this kaleidoscope of identities alone, one might already be able to see that Muslim American women are neither the same as non-Muslim American women nor one another. Rather, we are a rainbow of sects, practices, beliefs, and values. Under the umbrella of our general commonality, we differ widely.

The following essays will provide some insight into our collective and individual personal stories and concretely affirm our diversity. What you'll find in this book is multifold: a glimpse into our lives; emotion; stark honesty; inspiration; and above all, the realization that although our lives perhaps differ from yours, you will relate to us in the moments that we are most vulnerable, most introspective, and most *human*.

In this book, you'll meet Rashida, the eldest of fourteen children and the first Muslim woman elected to the Michigan legislature; Asma, a lawyer who struggles with Islamic feminism; Mona, who realizes her own fierce strength in the face of obstacles when she must defend her hijab to those closest to her; Hebah, who crafts her own brand of Muslim feminism and proudly passes it down to her daughter; Hadia, whose beautifully poetic prose evokes her struggle to bridge the worlds between her Jordanian, Islamic, and American roots; Nyla, an aspiring fashion designer who believes modesty is beautiful; and Rabea, who evokes the fluidity and purity of water to describe her approach to Islam and her own identity.

This is just a handful of the amazing women who share their stories with you. Our journeys and our stories haven't ended, and our conversations with ourselves and each other will continue even past the pages of this book. We hope you will enjoy your own journey through this book and you will be as inspired by these essays as we have been.

Hill Diaries
by Yusra Tekbali

Yusra Tekbali is a freelance journalist and blogger. Born in Woodland, California to Libyan parents, she graduated from the University of Arizona with degrees in journalism and Near Eastern studies. Yusra speaks Arabic and Spanish fluently. After college, she spent time in Washington, DC, where she worked as a staff assistant in the United States House of Representatives, volunteered with The Arab American Institute, and was elected to serve as a board member of the American-Arab Anti-Discrimination Committee. She also reported on Libyan women for the National Youth Council while living in Libya. Yusra blogs for Muslimah Media Watch, *and her work has appeared in* The Tripoli Post, The Arizona Daily Star, Chicago Public Radio, The Washington Diplomat, Al Jazeera English, The Arab American News, CNN, Global Post, *and* IslamOnline.Net. *Yusra is a certified Zumba instructor and a natural performer, with a background in theater, gymnastics, cheerleading, and dance. Her blog 7 Obsessions is a collection of spoken-word poems chronicling the complexities of being an Arab Muslim feminist in the contemporary world. Yusra was the only Libyan selected to compete in the Miss Arab USA Pageant 2011.*

I've always wanted to be an actress—a profession not strongly encouraged in the traditional Arab-American community in which I grew up. As my uncle would say, "We're being bombed left and right, and you want to be the next Soad Hosny![1]" That was 2003, and he was referring to the US invasion of Iraq. Around that time, I was in high school and becoming more politically active, staging local rallies, and volunteering with the Arab Anti-Discrimination Committee. Five years later—a month after graduating college—I put my acting plans on hold and moved to Washington, DC, to work for my representative in Congress. My little brother said I'd fit in because "DC is like Hollywood for ugly people."

Indeed, it was hard not be starstruck the first time I saw Senator John McCain in the Senate trolley or former House Speaker Nancy Pelosi and her entourage waltz past me in National Statuary Hall. And how could I forget the time archetypal villain and former Vice President Dick Cheney smirked at tourists snapping pictures as he escorted the Electoral College to the House Chamber. Despite regular run-ins with the rich and powerful, I felt more like an outsider than an A-lister as an Arab-American Muslim working in Congress.

Consider my conversation with Bill, a constituent who called Congresswoman Gabrielle Giffords's office after the House passed The American Recovery and Reinvestment Act of 2009 (aka the economic stimulus bill):

"The Office of Congresswoman Gabrielle Giffords," I answered with as much cheer as I could muster for what felt like the 900th call that hour.

"Yes, who am I speaking with?" asked Bill, in a croaky voice.

"This is Yusra, the staff assistant."

"Yuza?," Bill asked, incredulous.

"Yus-ra, sir. Can I help you?"

---

[1] The late Egyptian actress known as the "Cinderella of Arab cinema."

"Yuzzaaa." After a long pause, he asked "What kind of name is that?"

"It's Arabic. My parents named me after—"

"Arabic!" Angry grunting preceded a dial tone.

The origin of my name offended Bill, and his "I-don't-even-want-to-talk-to-you-because-you're-Arab" attitude offended me. Thinking about it later that afternoon, I realized this awkward exchange had occurred because Bill associates Arabs and Arab culture with Islamic extremism.

This train of thought is contagious. It's often spread by our media, and it also affects some members of Congress—particularly in matters of foreign policy, as on January 9, 2009, when the House passed H. Res. 34, a one-sided bill that ignored the escalating death toll in Gaza and reinforced the US stance on Israel's right to defend itself.

I remember listening indignantly to Representative Brad Sherman speak on the House floor, saying, "Hamas proudly waves the banner of genocide and ethnic cleansing." I wondered if he really believed the words he was saying—even as Israel continued to wage its campaign of violence, killing 1,000 Palestinians during the first nineteen days of fighting.

In our office, conversations about what was happening in Gaza were minimal. Our chief of staff and legislative director briefly discussed the situation the morning my congresswoman would sign her name to the bill.

"I'm concerned we [the US] didn't even sign the UN resolution. I mean, why wouldn't we do that?" one of them asked.

"Oh, we never sign those. And we never question Israel. That's how it always goes."

That was the end of their conversation. Bleak, I tried to tune it out and return to work but found myself unable to peel my eyes from *The Washington Post*. Plastered across the front page was a photo of emaciated Palestinian children found next to their mother's corpses. I tried my best to blink back the tears, worried someone might ask why I cared.

A few weeks later, a "Dear Colleague" letter titled "Beware of CAIR" was circulated around Congress. The memo, signed by four Republican members of the House, urged Congress to avoid meeting with the Council on Islamic Relations (CAIR) because of its supposed links to Hamas. The letter cited as evidence a story from a notoriously anti-Muslim source: *The Investigative Project on Terrorism.*

January was one of the loneliest and most depressing months I've spent on the Hill. I sought comfort by having lunch with an Arab friend, who was drafting an alternative bill for Representative Dennis Kucinich. This one actually recognized the humanitarian crisis in Gaza and called on both sides to end the ceasefire.

Her resolve was inspiring, and it reaffirmed my belief in the system as a means of change. After all, I work in Congress because I believe in democracy and the American way of governance. When I walk through the halls of the Capitol building, in the footsteps of white, Christian men, I'm reminded of the Declaration of Independence and the values America was founded on. I feel patriotic because I believe in those principles, in justice and equality for all. America has a troubled past, with several painful hiccups—the past eight years not excluded—but it also has an admirable history of supporting human rights, and I'm proud to have inherited that history.

When I'm roaming the Capitol's halls and the streets of Washington, I'm reminded of my US history class in elementary school and all that I learned about our country. I am reminded of the time I dressed up as a Native American for a school play and sang "America the Beautiful." Every time I walk by Alexander Hamilton's statue, I remember standing around with friends in high school discussing an essay question on the AP history exam that asked us to compare Hamilton's philosophical ideals with those of Thomas Jefferson, another man I admire. The historical significance of the Capitol reinforces what I learned in school. Working in proximity to it reminds me how America's history continues to shape my identity.

Throughout my life, I have never felt like my ethnicity or religion clashed with the love I have for America. Even when my family and I would visit Libya (my parent's birthplace and the land of my ancestors) during summer vacations, I longed to return home to the familiar country where I grew up. It's not that I think America is perfect or superior to anywhere else, but the comfort of a culture that is a hybrid of many other cultures makes it too endearing to leave for very long. September 11 may have triggered questions about my faith, but it didn't make me question whether or not I was American. Some people notoriously disagreed. They still do.

I recently took a call from Alan Smith, who was complaining about the economy, the immigrants, and the Fairness Doctrine. Then he said, "Yeah, tell the congresswoman to oppose abortion because if not, the Muslims will overpopulate and take over."

"What's wrong with that?" I replied somewhat sarcastically. "America will still be America if there are more Muslims running around."

It took me ten minutes to calm him down and assure him I'd taken down every single word of his comments.

The presence of American Muslims and Arab-Americans on the Hill is steadily rising as our community begins to establish itself politically. I was grateful for the support I found in the Congressional Muslim Staffers Association (CMSA), a group of Muslims who work in different capacities on the Hill. Through CMSA, I met American Muslims with experience in DC, and I began to feel more confident with my identity.

During the holy month of Ramadan, CMSA organized a Congressional dinner. I invited my coworkers to attend the dinner. I also made an effort to perform my prayers on time, stepping into the congresswoman's office or the supply room across the hall for five or ten minutes.

One afternoon, my coworker walked into the supply room and saw me praying. She excused herself and began to walk out, but I called her name and told her it was okay, explaining that prayer reminded me why I was fasting. It wasn't awkward, and it felt good to know I didn't have to hide my faith at work.

To be an Arab-American Muslim in American politics is to some degree paradoxical—not aided by the wars in Iraq and Afghanistan, the crimes of Guantanamo Bay and Abu Ghraib, the wireless taps … or the struggle to prove the fundamental humanity of the Palestinians.

Sometimes, it feels like I am racing against a clock that always reads 9:11. Yet, as more Arab-Americans and Muslims join the ranks of Congress and aspire to serve their nation (as Rep. Keith Ellison and Rep. André Carson are doing), the more difficult it will be to associate Arabs and Islam with terrorism.

"I think Rahm Emanuel is kind of good-looking," I said one evening to my friend Matt, a legislative correspondent from Los Angeles.

"Isn't that like blasphemy because you're an Arab Muslim and he's an Israeli Jew?" he quipped.

This prompted Matt's friend (whom I'd never met before) to joke, "An Arab in Congress?! Do Capitol police know?"

Thirty years from now, maybe conversations like this will lose their cultural significance.

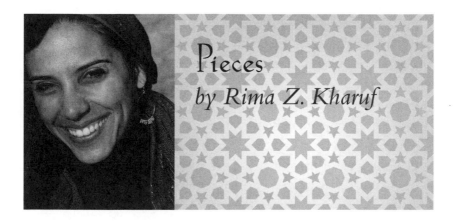

Pieces
by Rima Z. Kharuf

Rima Z. Kharuf was born and raised in Southern California. She currently teaches special education at a public school and enjoys hiking, learning about social justice issues, and earning frequent flyer miles visiting her family. Rima received her master's in counseling from California State University, Fullerton, as well as a master's in education and human development from The George Washington University. She and her husband live in Northern Virginia.

There are pieces of me
that stand on mountains
that sparkle
in tide pools
that contemplate
in deserts
that glisten
in city lights
but the whole of me
lies everywhere
and nowhere
at once.

If someone were to ask, "Who are you?" I might say I am a Palestinian American Muslim born and raised in Southern California and a descendant of refugees. I might tell them I love hiking, taking walks, learning people's stories, working with children, listening to music. I might also tell them that even though I can't draw or sing to save my life, I believe I have the soul of an artist. To describe who I am is to describe all of my fragmented pieces; they belong in several places, yet not wholly anywhere. God says in the Qur'an, "And on Earth there are signs for those with certainty, and in yourselves, will you not see?" (20–21:50).

My journey to find peace and wholeness has been intertwined with my relationship to nature. Although I did not begin to holistically understand my faith until recently, I unwittingly sought the guidance of God throughout my life by connecting with His presence on earth. This connection has helped me put the pieces of my Muslim identity together. My innate inclination to be in nature was, in reality, my subconscious desire to follow the *fitra* (innate desire) to be near God.

Talk to the Animals

As a child, I was drawn to nature. I believed I could communicate with animals. With a gentle touch of my hand, Lara, our German Shepherd guard dog, would stop barking at whoever was at the door and sit peacefully at my side. With Lara often tagging along, I explored the brush on the hills surrounding my house, finding "rare" insects and shoving them under microscopes. When I felt like losing all of my senses, I would hold my hands tightly across my chest and roll down the grassy hills in our neighborhood park. Dizzy, I would stand up, everything still spinning as I smelled the soil and freshly cut grass and felt the earth's dampness on my clothes. I would often run down those same hills flying kites. Watching the wind lift my little plastic diamond, I was amazed that something so small and insignificant could look so grand and beautiful.

I felt most at peace while immersed in nature. Consciously, however, my understanding of my faith was muddled. At Sunday school, we learned mainly about what we were and were not allowed to do. I knew that as a Muslim, I was supposed to believe in the Prophet Muhammad (peace and blessings upon him) and I was not allowed to eat pork. I knew we had two major holidays, during which I got money from my parents. I knew that at the mosque I had to cover my hair. We were taught rituals without meaning or context, expected to do things for the sake of not being punished by God. We were not taught about the Prophet—how he had lived his early childhood in the deserts of Mecca and had spent time meditating in nature, where the Qur'an was revealed to him only after countless hours of reflection in the cave. At that age, I did not connect my desire to be near the creations of God to a desire to be near God. All I knew was that in nature I felt peace. In the years to come, I would search for that same feeling within my faith.

Among my peers at school, I was painfully shy and reserved. One of the few brown kids in a mostly white neighborhood, I rarely spoke up in class and tried my best to be invisible. My tan skin and dark features were, in my mind, a deficiency. I often wished I had a "normal" name, yellow streaked hair, and lightly sunburned skin. Despite my efforts to not be noticed, curious and ignorant individuals often called attention to my differences. I was frequently having to explain that yes, my tan was natural and I guess I was lucky to have it all year round, and no, I had never ridden a camel. Frequently they would ask, "Where are you from?"—increasingly making me feel that I did not belong there and that I was an "other." The only place I truly felt at ease was when I was running around outdoors with Lara next to me, the world spinning around, the smell of wet earth in my nostrils.

Tide Pools and Sunsets

In my early adolescent years, my understanding of Islam remained fractured and incomplete. At that point in my life, my Islam consisted of ritual obligations I did not deeply connect with or understand. Nature was my refuge, my source of peace and balance. I spent my days taking long walks around my neighborhood, my evenings stargazing, and my summers volunteering as a junior naturalist. I took trips to local tide pools, where I poked sea anemones as I felt their sticky tentacles suctioning around my fingers. I hiked the fragrant sage hills, rubbing the leaves between my fingers and piercing cacti with pocketknives to find hidden succulence. I helped clean a local estuary that reeked of sludge and the careless disregard of people. I created works of art out of twigs, leaves, berries, and pinecones, crafting beauty from my surroundings. Those summers, I learned how to use my senses, how to discover the beauty around me, and how to appreciate the splendor in diversity. Years later, I would come to understand this as a form of worship.

In high school, I searched for a tangible relationship with God by establishing regular prayer. Prayer was difficult. I wanted so much to feel connected, but I often struggled to remain in a state of awareness and consciousness of God. My favorite part of prayer was the moment when, upon completion, I would sit on my prayer rug, raising my hands up and just talking to my Creator, asking Him for guidance, mercy, and blessings. There was something powerful about feeling I was conversing with God. It made me think of another time I would feel compelled to make *dua*, or supplication—while I was in nature. My favorite spot was on a bench near my home that overlooked the tide pools. From my vantage point, the tide pools looked deceivingly small and simplistic: jaggedly curvaceous rocks holding little pools of water. I knew, however, that in reality there was an amazingly complex ecosystem living in the shallow pools of those rocks.

Like the scattered pools, I felt more complex than I thought possible for anyone to understand—fragmented, disconnected, and without a sense of wholeness. I wasn't sure who I was, but I often asked God to make me into the person I wanted to be: strong, confident, artistic, beautiful, and most importantly, whole. Subconsciously, it was my fitra that drew me towards God as I reflected on His creation. It was at this point in my life that I began to bridge together my ideas of nature and worship.

During my junior year of college, September 11 occurred. Being one of the few Muslims on our campus, I had the opportunity to speak on behalf of my faith. I sat on campus panels educating people about and defending Islam. Over and over again, I found myself lumped into the category of "them." It became increasingly important to me that I figure out my own individual relationship with Islam. I decided to study the religion more, and in doing so, I began to understand its deeply spiritual elements. Once again, I drew a parallel to the reverence I felt when surrounded by nature. The brilliant smoggy Los Angeles sunsets that streaked the skies with violet, magenta, and mandarin reminded me daily that amidst the murky passages of life's journey comes the vividness of majesty.

Mountains

In 2007, I moved to Washington, DC, somewhat unexpectedly. Having just completed my master's degree in counseling, I was visiting friends and family in the DC area. I ended up canceling my return ticket to California. I had met so many kindred spirits: artists, teachers, environmentalists, lawyers, soul-searchers, philosophers, human rights advocates—all beautiful in their uniqueness. I had never been around such intensely passionate, dedicated, and inspiring individuals. Through a dear friend of mine—one of the founders of DC Green Muslims—I became involved in connecting Islam to environmental issues. We had numerous discussions on the intertwining of God-consciousness with the environment, and we worked in the community doing service projects. My humble participation in this group helped me connect two distinct elements in my life that I had only partially associated in the past. Although I still perceived my identity as fragmented, I started to experience my spirituality as interwoven with my relationship to nature.

It was later that year when I climbed my first physical mountain. Accompanied by my good friends Jasmine and Ibrahim, I steadily made my way up Old Rag Mountain in the Shenandoah Valley, approximately a four-and-a-half–mile hike each way. Ibrahim insisted we keep moving so we could catch the view before the sun began to set. I was huffing and puffing the last two miles as we climbed up boulders, stumbled over thick tree roots, and adjusted to the altitude change. A few times, I wanted to give up. I was tired, cold, and worried about the impending sunset. A few experienced hikers coming down the mountain asked us if we were equipped for the dark and bitter cold nightfall would bring. I started to get nervous, but Ibrahim assured us we would be well on our way before it got too dark.

Once we reached the top, I forgot about how much I had struggled to get to that point. I paused, inhaled, and exhaled. Reflecting amidst the glory of God, I was silenced by the beauty before me, awestruck at the sight of millions of trees. I was most struck by the thought that each of these individual trees had gone through the exact same processes as all of the other trees, their leaves all changing to the same shade of yellow in unison. I saw myself as one of those trees, understanding my lifelong search for spirituality and the numberless hours of reflection serving to prepare me for the different seasons of life. I realized that even though my struggle is unique to my experience, I was part of a forest. I felt connected to the world around me, no longer fragmented. I began to understand myself, my life, and my journey as a means to cultivating my love for *As-Salam, An-Nur, Al-Wadud* (The Bestower of Peace, The Light, The Loving One.)

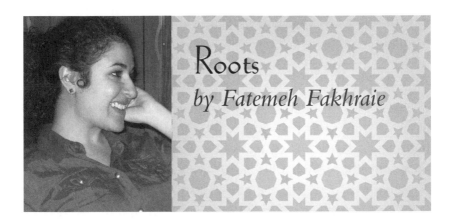

Roots
by Fatemeh Fakhraie

Fatemeh Fakhraie is an editor, author, and blogger who explores various issues from her perspective as an American-Iranian Muslim woman. She writes about Islamic feminism, Islam, politics, and race for several online and print outlets, including Racialicious, Bitch magazine, *and* AltMuslimah. *She founded Muslimah Media Watch in 2007 and currently serves as editor-in-chief.*

Ma gave me this guilty little line, "I never get to spend enough time with you. You only ever visit for a few days."

She promised to take me shopping and to lunch at my favorite places, as if they had to bribe me. When she said she'd like to buy me some clothes, I got angry. Did she really think I'd come just to get some new clothes? Then, guilty. Did she really think I wouldn't come unless they took me to my favorite restaurants?

If I go visit them, I won't get to catch my brother's eye as we simultaneously roll our eyes at our irritating parents. I won't have a partner in the criminal fun we poke at our parents. He will work instead, and he won't come home to make me laugh or say things that bother me because he likes to push my buttons. He won't come home because he hates the place, just like I do. He feels cramped. Just like I do. Why sleep in a crowded childhood home when you can stay in your spacious apartment forty-five minutes away?

I hate going back to that little place I've outgrown. I hate seeing everything the same—dusty and stagnant. It makes me antsy, itchy, and irritated. I wish I could clean the house, throw out old history books we don't need, and enroll my parents in pottery classes. Instead, I tear my hair out thinking about how small they live. And how comfortable they are with it. Why live on the creaky springs of harder times? Why live with neighbors who have died? Why live with a fish tank that nurtures only algae?

When I go back, everything looks the same, and this tricks me. Everything cannot be the same forever. Baba's hair has so many gray strands now. The skin around Ma's eyes is so much more wrinkled. But since everything there feels and looks the same, I am lulled into thinking it is only I who has aged. I have been outside—growing, living, and aging—while my parents have been sealed in a vacuum.

Baba and I are so similar, it's hard to get along sometimes. It's easier to burrow into our ideas and piles of books than to figure each other out. We are cut from the same cloth, but our experiences have taken us to two different places. Searching for himself and a better life drew Baba away from the Islamic Republic of Iran; searching for myself and my roots draws me nearer to it. Yet in reality, it is not the republic I am drawn to. Rather, I am trying to get nearer to my father through this land where my ancestors are buried.

My mother is a strong woman, and it's from her that I learned to be strong myself. When personal strength isn't enough, she always told me, "It's good to have faith." After I learned to lean on faith, my parents worried because my faith was more public than theirs—they worried I would turn into something they didn't recognize. They worried perhaps their Fatemeh would become *Fatemeh Komando*.[1]

They worry about me, and I worry about them. I worry about Baba when he falls asleep in front of the TV, and his snoring is so loud I want to put a pillow over his face. I worry about how small Ma looks when I get irritated and accidentally say something that hurts her feelings.

I worry they will die. What will I do if they die? Who will make us laugh by teasing Ma if Baba is gone? Who will tickle Baba until he squeals if Ma is gone? Who else will laugh at their own jokes or call because they miss me?

Baba doesn't take care of himself, his father had a heart attack at this age, he doesn't exercise. Downwinders Syndrome could give Ma another type of cancer, what if she breaks something …

Who will take me to Iran? Who will take me to see my grand-parents' graves?

How can anyone really know me if they don't know I have the same laugh and the same short temper as my Baba? How can anyone understand exactly why sounding like my mother freaks me out if they've never met her?

God, sweet God.

I think to myself sometimes that if I cry for their deaths now, God won't take them from me. Like reverse psychology. I am so fearful for their deaths. If one goes, the other one will, too. Maybe a body would remain behind, but Baba would never laugh that way again, or Ma's eyes would be even paler than now.

I don't even know how to talk to them about this. "Ma, if Baba dies, will I have to take care of you? Will my heart break every day when I see only half of you sitting there?"

---

[1] "Fatemeh Komando" is a slang term used for female members of Iran's police force. These women are best known for enforcing Iran's dress code, which states that all women must cover their hair and bodily curves.

They have sunk so deeply into their ruts. I worry because I know only something huge can pull them out, but everything huge has scary names like "cardiac episode" or "end of remission."

Taking care of one's aging parents is a Muslim duty, an Iranian duty, an American duty. I feel this duty keenly, even when my American upbringing teaches me to focus on only myself and my future. My parents have not hinted at or voiced this idea. My brother and I just know it's our responsibility. Our parents took care of us when we were small and weak; in return, we shall take care of them when they are weak. It's repaying the ultimate debt.

I don't need them like some others need their parents. I don't talk to them every day. But I need them to be there, falling asleep in front of the TV, teasing each other when they call me to complain about whatever my brother's doing. I need them to call and talk about the stupid weather and tell me silly local gossip about nobodies and old buildings I'd forgotten about long before they were bought by a new owner. I don't know why I need them, but I need them.

I want to buy my mother a pedicure. Paradise is at her feet, but I haven't done shit to deserve it myself. At least I'll be able to look at the pretty toenails I bought her as I'm sliding down to pseudo-hell where daughters who don't know how to love their parents go.

I sigh because I'm gonna pack up my fucking guilt and go there. And you know what will happen? Baba will snore too loudly in front of the TV. I will watch Ma age as she talks about work. I'll feel cramped and frustrated because that little space isn't enough for me anymore. My brother will work too much, and we'll only see him when we visit the Iranian market and go shopping at the mall near his apartment. His girlfriend, who doesn't understand us at all, will come to dinner, and I will try so hard to be nice to her, even though I'm horrible at hiding my discomfort. I will spend too much time online because I'm busy trying to find a job.

Yet "fixing" my relationship with my parents doesn't occur to me. My relationship with my parents isn't broken. It isn't something that can be fixed or changed: I am the obedient daughter, and they are the authoritative parents. We are from two different generations. In their generation, parents did not stop being parents to become friends. Parents from their generation are advice-givers and problem-fixers, not confidantes or bar buddies.

The conflicts arising from these generational and cultural gaps are perpetual and inevitable. They will always happen, and I will always be frustrated by them. But I will always love my parents, and I will always need them. It's the same two-sided coin many other parent-child relationships have. With us, the coin just seems to be in motion more often.

And so I'll go shopping with Ma and push her to try on new clothes because she deserves them more than her vain daughter. I'll sit next to Baba while he falls asleep on the couch and snores so loudly I can't hear the TV. I'll go, because I know they need me as much as I need them.

Half and Half
by Nousheen Yousuf-Sadiq

Nousheen Yousuf-Sadiq received her bachelor's degree from the University of Illinois at Chicago. She majored in history with a double minor in religious studies and gender and women's studies. Nousheen earned her master's degree in religious studies from Boston University, where she focused on women in Islam. After graduating, she taught a religion course at a Chicago-area community college. She now lives in Philadelphia with her husband and is currently working as a freelance editor. Nousheen aspires to attain her PhD in religion and teach at the university level. She wishes to give a voice to marginalized peoples and help bridge gaps in understanding within and between the diverse Muslim community and surrounding American populations.

I walked into the local coffee shop down the street from my Boston apartment to grab a chai latté and read my paper. After taking my order, the enthusiastic cashier asked, "Would you like nonfat milk in your chai?" Stunned, my immediate thought was, "Woman, do I look like I drink nonfat milk?" But after taking a moment, I responded, "Actually, make it with half and half." That's right. I ordered half cream, half whole milk. Full, wonderful flavor.

I knew the typical customer at this popular café chain would say "brevé," but I purposely named my choice of milk to make a point.

Waiting for my drink to steam, I wondered why the cashier had automatically assumed I wanted skim milk. Was it because I was a woman? Must every female be a calorie-counting, salad-binging carbaphobe? In this size-obsessed world, I took quite a while to become comfortable with my own body, and I didn't appreciate the assumption that I was on the bread-burning bandwagon like so many women seemed to be.

Escaping advice for improvement seemed virtually impossible, but I had discovered a simple yet empowering way to rise above the sea of criticism. The secret lay in my decision to wear hijab, the Islamic headscarf—a feminist strategy I used to become comfortable in my own skin and to master the delicate mix of my American and Muslim identities.

For as long as I could remember, the message I received from magazines, television, and music videos was, "You're only as good as you are pretty." This message didn't come in such a direct form, but rather a constant barrage of subtle and not-so-subtle hints. First, a frontal attack: the cover of a tween magazine telling me how to shed pounds. Next, coverage of a designer's newest line, in which anorexia is apparently the new black. Then the ambush: the third diet supplement commercial in a row. This wasn't random advertising—it was full-on psychological warfare. With the beauty bar set so high, it's no wonder all women are assumed to be self-conscious about their weight. The acceptable body shape changes with every season. With so much inconsistency, the only constant I experienced when I was younger was my dependence on others' approval.

As an American woman, I had an insatiable desire to feel confident with who I was and how I looked. I was brought up with an idealized sense of what a woman should be: my generation's feminine mystique. The perfect woman was articulate, strong, and in control of herself and her own life. I was none of these—least of all the latter. Searching for excuses, I continually blamed my timidity on my appearance. I was convinced that if I looked different, I would be a completely different person and find the confidence I was searching for.

As a Muslim, I wanted to meet the requirements of my faith. This included adopting the Islamic standards of modest dress. I was always under the impression these goals of finding confidence and satisfying my religious self ran counter to one another, which left me hopelessly confused. I wanted to wear hijab, but I was unsure of the effects it would have on my life, my future career, and most immediately, my confidence.

Seeking acceptance, I used to wear revealing clothing to compensate for my inability to feel pretty. Yet whenever I received the male attention I so longed for, it didn't give me any sense of self-worth, and it definitely didn't make me feel pretty. Instead, I felt objectified, offended, even violated by passing comments. Although a skimpy wardrobe did not yield the result I was looking for, I thought dressing in accordance with Islamic law would only aggravate my insecurities by restricting my choice of clothing. While not wearing hijab, I was consumed with concerns about how others would judge my appearance. It was a private decision with public ramifications. I often wondered whether I, a young American woman, could take ownership of my Muslim identity to the degree that I would quite literally wear it on my sleeve. The decision to wear hijab meant my two identities would have to coexist harmoniously in my dress.

The summer before I started college, I traveled with a youth group to Iran, where women are legally required to wear the headscarf and modest dress in public. I had already worn hijab from time to time at religious events, so its imposition was nothing more than a minor inconvenience. My experience in the

Islamic Republic served as a spiritual awakening for me in many ways. I now felt comfortable expressing my Muslim identity. It was time for a fresh start—including a new wardrobe.

I began wearing hijab on my first day of college. During my first class at the University of Illinois at Chicago, I was too busy scanning the room to see who was looking at me to concentrate on the lecture. It was not because I was paranoid about my headscarf. Never before had I realized how much I'd allowed my looks to speak for who I was. In those introductory moments to college life, I literally began to feel my internal qualities being pushed to the fore and my external qualities being tossed aside.

This unfamiliar feeling was frightening because, like most young Americans, I had no idea who I was. I truly believed the headscarf, being such a visible marker of my faith, would bring more attention to my physical appearance—not who I was on the inside. Instead, the opposite occurred. I was forced to discover myself because I was no longer hiding behind a façade of cute clothes and new hairstyles.

To my surprise, my confidence surged. As insecure as I'd been without hijab, I became equally as secure with my hijab, and I felt something I'd never felt before: control. Without hijab, society's standards of beauty dictated how I presented myself to the world and, by extension, how I thought of myself when I didn't measure up. When following the Islamic dress code, I had control over who did and didn't look at me, who did and didn't touch me. I had a greater sense of authority over how people viewed me because for the first time, people were not seeing my outer appearance—they were seeing *me*.

I also went from just caring about my image to caring about my health. I could eat without guilt because I no longer subscribed to society's menu for female eating. It wasn't until after my decision to wear hijab that I felt liberated and my identity as a Muslim solidified. My desire to not be objectified was rooted in my faith, which taught me that physical appearance is something private, even sacred, and it is the internal qualities that are to be shared with the world. Only after I started hijab did I come to know its true value.

Hijab served as the catalyst for me to develop my character, gain confidence in whom I had become, and attain autonomy over my body and my life. Since achieving control over oneself is the essence of feminism, I unknowingly adopted a mechanism that facilitated reaching both of my goals simultaneously. It was refreshing and liberating to allow my internal qualities to become the standard by which I was measured. My hijab, my feminist strategy, allowed me to be on a more equal footing with men because my physical appearance was a much smaller component. People no longer saw my appearance but my intelligence and personality. Unlike some of my colleagues, who dressed in modest or conservative clothing to be taken seriously at work, I felt hijab allowed me the same ability without compromising my femininity or fashion sense. As a Muslim, finding the strength to wear the headscarf was incredibly important to me. Although my decision was initially driven by my religion, both the spiritual and social benefits ultimately gave it meaning.

It makes sense that I ordered half and half with my chai latté that morning. After all, I am made up of two parts: my Muslim and American identities. My Muslim identity defined half of my personality, character, and individuality, while the other half has been determined by my experience growing up as an American. The balance of the two makes me who I am: an American woman who has discovered her hijab is the greatest beauty secret of all.

In Search of
Fatima and Taqwa
by Maria M. Ebrahimji

*Maria M. Ebrahimji is a journalist and executive editorial pro-
ducer for CNN, where she is responsible for guest coverage and
story planning for the network's special events and breaking news
programming. Maria is a member of the Asian American Journalists
Association and serves on the boards of the Atlanta Press Club
and Tau Chapter of Alpha Chi Omega. She holds a bachelor's
degree in mass communications from Brenau Women's College and
a master's in international affairs from Georgia State University.
While born in Westminster, Maryland, as the eldest daughter of
East African immigrants, Maria was raised in Northeast Georgia
and proudly embraces Southern hospitality. Her spare time is spent
traveling the world, hiking, running, and being an idealist. Maria
currently lives in lives in Atlanta, Georgia.*

I'll never forget what that sheikh said to me in Yemen. He was
well-educated and savvy about the world, certainly opinion-
ated, and willing to engage me in talk of current events as if I
were one of his British chums from university. But when the
conversation turned to personal matters—that of seeking a suit-
able husband and what I hoped to do with my life—his jolliness

turned to sheer matter-of-factness. His prescription for my life's success was simple yet forceful: consider staying home more, traveling less, perhaps letting some of my career go to find "a good Muslim husband."

My women's-college–educated mind urged me to stare him down and set him straight. Clearly, he had not been educated in this century and hadn't heard about the era of women's liberation. I felt my cloud falling as I shrank quietly back in my seat. I remained silent partly because of the embarrassment I felt for my parents—who had been sitting next to me during this exchange and were equally aghast—and partly because I was unwilling to further ignite the uncomfortable tension in the car. The desert was hot enough already.

I respected this sheikh and until he uttered such statements, I had been equally impressed by his tenacity. He had moved from India to Britain for education before leaving all things Western behind to come to Yemen. While I see Yemen as the most beautiful, people-filled place in the world, it certainly doesn't offer luxury or efficiency. Yet the sheikh was here, serving and ministering to the local community and worshippers like us who had traveled from afar. His service alone was enough to make one feel humbled, but his comments were what made me feel small, less-respected, and in some ways, less worthy of being the fearless and self-supporting woman I thought I had become. Personal sacrifices of time, emotion, or money I have always lived with, but never once had I been told to pare back *myself* to get what I wanted in life. All at once, this aroused in me both a resoluteness and curiosity.

In advising me how to find a good Muslim husband, was this sheikh trying to tell me how to be a good Muslim *woman*? Were my free spirit, independence, feminist thinking, and "Americanness" preventing me from being a model *Muslim* woman? Should I give up one identity to fit comfortably into another? Did it matter? Couldn't they coexist? These thoughts followed me all the way home.

I consulted my upbringing. Our family represented an anomaly in the small Southern suburb where I grew up. Despite outside influences, however, I knew my faith from the outset. I never questioned my place in it. I was a Muslim girl who was also Indian and American and as one elementary school teacher put it, "white with a very nice tan." I did not wear my Muslim-ness on my sleeve. Nor did I choose to hide it in any way. I wore jeans and shorts to class, climbed mountains, swam in the lake, fasted at school, prayed at home, and even went to my junior prom with a non-Muslim boy. None of this I found to conflict with the person I was: a Muslim girl. I was taught to believe in the major tenets of Islam, to diligently practice them, and to seek God's guidance in every decision and action I undertook. My inside belief, my *taqwa* or God consciousness, made me Muslim at the core.

I reflected on my education and transition to my career. I recall my refugee father encouraging education as the only way to become someone in America. He had supported my mass communications major even though it was unlike the "respectable" career paths my other Indian "uncles" encouraged him to have me follow.

Empowered by my women's college education and armed with the notion that all things were possible, I set out on the career path I had always wanted. Once I emerged from the comfortable bubble of sisterhood that had enveloped me and began to see myself in the real world, I also recognized this new opportunity to define myself as I wanted to be defined. I introduced myself by using the more Indian pronunciation of my name. I stopped wearing shorts. I grew more into my Muslim and South Asian identity and refined my American-ness. I learned Arabic and read the Qur'an more. I found myself speaking up more and attempting to correct any misreporting about my faith. I looked for positive Muslim stories to tell after 9/11 in hopes that others would be able to recognize the good I saw in my faith.

I also began asking myself questions I wasn't informed enough to answer. Is a good Muslim woman to be submissive or independent, strong or weak? A willing bearer of children, a good wife, or a dutiful cultivator of her faith, her body, her soul? Is wearing hijab to mosque and then taking it off at work hypocritical? If I hadn't completed reading the Qur'an or never made up those missed childhood fasts, would I be less Muslim? If I repented, was I any more Muslim? If I shook people's hands in meetings or allowed my voice or face to be heard or seen by men, across airwaves or on television, was I less chaste? Was I less of a Muslim woman? Was I Muslim enough?

After that trip to Yemen, those same questions ran through my head like a television ticker. I became increasingly conscious of my inability to answer these questions and fixated on finding one answer that would complete and wholly sustain me. The questions pounded inside of me. It was my own internal *ma'atam* (rhythmic beating of the chest), a sound that had mesmerized me as a girl attending mosque during the holy month of Muharram.

The first time I saw my mother cry was when we performed that ritual in mosque. It was a profound yet simple act of faith, but her emotion and that of the women surrounding me became increasingly high when Fatima, the daughter of the prophet Muhammad, was recognized. Great tears of respect and celebration and sorrow were shed in recognition of her life.

Many times, in my own youthful naiveté, I had questioned how a woman who had seemed almost of legend, who had lived more than 1,000 years ago, could still inspire emotion among men and women alike. I now know why. As a foremother of

Islam and a timeless model of womanhood, she was the kind Muslim woman I knew I wanted to become. I was searching for the Fatima in myself.

While my outward appearance may suggest my faithfulness to the world, my real faith, my inner taqwa, is only known to God and me—as it should be. I feel comfortable shaking people's hands, male or female. I do not fixate on the trivial and instead focus on adhering to the basic tenets of Islam every day. I try to maintain inner taqwa at all times. I rely on the strength I find in my faith to help me continue with my career. I use my taqwa as a shield against those who question the "Islamic-ness" of my career or lifestyle. I stop worrying whether I am Muslim enough and concentrate on making sure I am conscious of my Muslim identity every day, whether by performing prayer or simply acknowledging thanks to God in my heart.

While I may not have fully come to terms with those television ticker questions, I find solace in Fatima's example, which informs and nourishes my own life experience.

I wonder how Fatima would have responded to the sheikh? His advice touched painfully on the question I'd been asking myself all my life: *Am I Muslim enough?*

I think Fatima would say to both the sheikh and me that all is possible. She protected her family and held her community together in times of great divisiveness; she stood up for her rights and her inheritance when her father died. She used the Qur'an as her guide. She was humble, honorable, knowledge-able, and wise. She was a loving daughter, loyal wife, and caring mother. Fatima's dreams were in her family, and she pursued and defended them. She maintained her inner taqwa, and she bore the qualities I see important in all women.

I can be who I want to be and still be like Fatima. The identity I inherited at birth I have come to embrace and refine as time passes. And while I can choose to pare myself down by choice or grow myself stronger through circumstance, I am no more or no less *Muslim* than I was in the beginning. What tormented me in the Yemen desert has only reaffirmed the writing of God on my solidly Muslim American Indian—independent—soul.

The Muslim
Feminist
by Hebah Ahmed

Hebah Ahmed was born in Chattanooga, Tennessee, to Egyptian immigrants. She attended a Catholic all-girls high school in Houston, Texas, before earning her bachelor's and master's degrees in mechanical engineering from Texas A&M University and the University of Illinois at Urbana-Champaign respectively. After several years in the corporate world, Hebah left to explore her spirituality and become a community activist and mother. She is married to Dr. Zayd Leseman, a professor at the University of New Mexico, and homeschools her two children. After September 11, 2001, Hebah began wearing hijab and niqab in response to a deepening love and understanding of Islam and modesty. She has founded two organizations: Daughterz of Eve, a Muslim youth club for girls, and Muslim Women's Outreach, which sponsors interfaith dialogues that build bridges and educate people about Islam and Muslim women. She is currently an associate writer for MuslimMatters.org.

Growing up, I was exposed to a double standard I had assumed was a genuine part of Islam. In my family and Muslim community, I noticed differences in the way sons and daughters were brought up. Boys and men were afforded a much greater free-dom than girls and women. Many of the Muslim women around me worked just as hard at their careers as their husbands, but it was the women who bore the brunt of the responsibilities when they returned home. They cooked, cleaned, and took care of the kids, while their husbands sat catatonic in front of the TV, issuing commands to their wives.

As a young child, I never saw my mother complain about her role in life. She had a master's degree in civil engineering, but I was scarcely aware of her background or skills. Rather than help around the house, I added to her load. I refused to wash my own dishes or pick up after myself, assuming she would take care of it all. At this point in life, I had not yet identified myself with my mother, nor had I begun to compare her present reality to my future one as a Muslim woman.

As I entered high school, I finally realized that when I married and had a family, my fate would probably be similar to that of my mother's. I rebelled, trying to convince my mother that she was doing too much and pleading with my father to do more. He would tell me this was what women were created for. He truly believed women had the desire and patience to cook, clean, and calm a screaming child—while men did not. I begged to differ. Internally, I began to develop arguments against his position, but I did not have the experience or confidence to boldly confront him. I was still developing my identity and preferred to take on an observer's perspective, mentally collecting data on the various ways families—Muslim and non-Muslim alike—operated.

Although my father subscribed to what I consider a tradi-tional view of women, he contradicted this view when it came to his daughters. He was the proud father of three intelligent girls, whom he constantly pushed to overachievement. My father repeatedly told me I could be the best at anything I did and to always aim high.

Once while in second grade, prior to the school's annual field day, my father gave me a pep talk about the race I was about to run.

"Make sure you set your goal to a point way beyond the finish line," he advised. "That will ensure that you run hard the entire race and finish strong. Most people set their sights on the finish line and then slow down as they near the end. If you look beyond, then you will always have an advantage." I did not yet realize I would refer to this analogy for the rest of my life.

My father was always asking about our schoolwork and our grades. One day, in third grade, I returned home with apprehension.

"Did you get that quiz back that you took yesterday?" he asked.

"Uh, yes," I said gloomily.

"What did you make?" he said with increasing concern.

"Um, well, it was hard."

"Okay, so what did you get?"

"Um ... uh ... I got a D."

"You got a *what*?!"

For the next month, my father jokingly nicknamed me "Captain D." Reminding me of my failure was his way of dissuading me from repeating my mistake. It worked. The nickname irritated me, but rather than getting upset or rebelling, I developed higher standards for myself and worked hard to regain my father's respect.

During my sophomore year at my Catholic all-girls high school, I received a letter inviting me to apply for early admission to college. Since the campus was five hours away, I assumed my parents would not even consider it. Not bothering to show my parents the letter, I resigned myself to the idea that this was going to be an unfulfilled opportunity. I was used to limits and strict rules from my parents, so I did not dwell on the letter for long, although I felt a profound sense of loss and disappointment.

As I was throwing the invitation away, my father asked me what it was. I told him, and he immediately encouraged me to apply and see what would happen. Completely shocked, I realized my father's deep love of education dwarfed his sexist views on women. The instantaneous switch from an overwhelming sense of loss to feelings of hope and support left me reeling, my mind racing with possibilities I had not yet allowed myself to entertain. I excitedly applied. A month later, I timidly showed my father the letter of acceptance. His deep pride in my achievements won out over my mother's concerned protests. At the age of fifteen, I was on my way to college!

As I wove my way through college, I was exposed to many different philosophies and worldviews. Having lived a relatively sheltered life, I was especially impressionable at that young age. I was thrust into a co-ed environment, where I witnessed the pitfalls of early sexual experimentation and drug abuse among my friends. This reaffirmed my Islamic beliefs on abstaining from drugs, alcohol, and premarital sex. I stayed up all night debating the merits of religion with atheists, who scoffed at my supposed naiveté and pushed me to defend my beliefs from a logical and philosophical perspective. I read academic books that attempted to define humanity's purpose and motivations, arguing about the differences between human-made and divine systems. All of these experiences were new to me, and in the end, they served to deepen my Islamic convictions.

My belief, however, was incomplete because I still found myself struggling with an internal conflict. I defined the Islamic view of women by my parents' relationship. They claimed they had been acting in line with Islam, and yet this meant a view of women I was not quite able to accept. I confronted the contradictions in my upbringing, searching for my true identity and role as a Muslim woman. This manifested itself as arguments with my father as I attempted to prove my parents wrong.

"When you marry, you will have to serve your husband just like your mother does," my father would say. This struck at the root of my identity. My father had raised me to always aim high—yet within the context of marriage, he was suddenly asking me to settle.

"But I don't want to live my life like Mom! My husband *will* pick up his plate when he finishes eating, and *he* will wash it! He'll change diapers, too!"

"If you keep thinking that way, you'll be divorced for sure," he responded.

How could my father tell me to be the best and push me to get the finest education money could buy—and then turn around and tell me my lot in life was to be subservient to some man?

My internal turmoil increased. I could not give up my Islamic identity. Not only did I have a very strong belief in God and His final revelation, but I also appreciated the many logical and beneficial aspects of the Islamic lifestyle. Nevertheless, I was deeply conflicted over my father's view of women, which he claimed were preached in Islam. I respected my father and was not yet mature enough to admit he could be mistaken or imperfect, so I couldn't simply reject his position. Instead, the conflict created a split personality inside me. At home, I upheld and acted on one set of beliefs in line with my father's teachings—fearing I would otherwise be turning my back on Islam or disappointing my father—while at school, I developed a more analytical and questioning attitude.

This conflicting value system came to a head in graduate school. I lived by myself, which gave me the time and confidence to really think through my life philosophy and goals. I always believed in the basic tenets of Islam: worshiping only one God, the Creator of all, and following the way of His prophets. It was the practical application and human example I struggled with. I began to attend weekly prayer services at the local *masjid* (mosque), where I met other Muslim girls. Many of them wore the hijab and had attended Islamic schools prior to college. Their conviction intrigued me, and I began to ask questions.

Zoha, who would later become a close friend, loaned me a book on the life of the prophet Muhammad—set 1,400 years ago. It was the first time I had ever read a book about him, and it changed my life.

As I read the pages, I felt my world had been turned upside-down. The manners the prophet Muhammad exhibited and the compassionate, giving manner in which he interacted with people repeatedly brought me to tears. I began comparing the Muslim men I knew to the prophet Muhammad, which left me confused and doubtful. Either the book was a lie, or somehow, the men I knew had veered way off track.

Then I began to read about a woman named Khadijah. The book described her as a forty-year-old woman of great nobility, a widow and wealthy businesswoman who employed men to take her goods and trade them abroad. After hiring the prophet Muhammad as one of her traders and observing his impeccable manners and actions, she sought him out in marriage. Although he was fifteen years her junior, he happily agreed to her proposal. They were the loves of each other's lives, and the accounts of their home life together would make any woman jealous.

As I read this story, I felt something changing inside of me. Tears gushed from my eyes and a deep sense of awe, relief, and empowerment overtook me. Could this be true? The wife of our revered prophet, the example for all men, was an older, wealthy businesswoman who had proposed marriage to him? Isn't this marriage really the example Muslim couples should be following?

"This is true feminism!" my mind screamed. "This is the missing piece—the solution to the contradiction I have been feeling in my belief. This is the religion I love!" I finally recognized that my father's view of women had been solely based on his cultural upbringing. The Islamic perspective—as represented in the Qur'an and life of the prophet Muhammad—was something different entirely. It was respectful, honoring, and completely validating. It was then that I swore to myself that if I ever had a daughter, I would name her Khadijah.

That profound epiphany was the beginning of my real journey to Islam. It was the point when I finally saw the difference between the cultural Islam I was raised in and the true Islam based on original texts. Visiting my Muslim relatives, I realized it was their ignorance of Islam and cultural attitudes that had created this inequality of the sexes. This ignorance had triggered such violent actions as honor killings and abuse of women in the Muslim world—behavior that contradicted the teachings of the Qur'an and the example set by the prophet Muhammad.

At last, I had achieved the inner peace that comes when you find synergy among your beliefs, logic, and relationships. I was flooded with a deep sense of liberation and relief. After sincerely searching and wading through the enormous pressures and conflicting perspectives of life, I finally felt comfortable in my own skin. I had found the truth: a faith I could fully submit to without hesitation or doubt, knowing my Creator understood me completely and gave me true guidance that would not fail me. This pushed me to commit to a life of learning and practicing Islam based on authentic sources and teachings rather than human-made systems that result in injustice and oppression.

It is this true Islam that I am now teaching my precious daughter, Khadijah.

And yes, my husband picks up his plate and washes it, ignoring my father's protests. And he's changed his fair share of dirty diapers.

Conquering Veils:
Gender and Islams
by Asma T. Uddin

Asma T. Uddin is the founder and editor-in-chief of altmuslimah. com. She is also an international law attorney with The Becket Fund for Religious Liberty, a public interest law firm based in Washington, DC. Asma's writing has appeared in Muslim Girl Magazine, Islamica Magazine, *altmuslim, beliefnet, and in* The Guardian's *"Comment is Free."* She is an expert panelist for the Washington Post/Newsweek *blog* On Faith, *and a contributor to* Huffington Post Religion, CNN Belief Blog, *and* Common Ground News. *Her scholarly work has been published in the* Rutgers Journal of Law and Religion, The Review of Faith & International Affairs, *and the* St. Thomas Law Review. *Asma has traveled throughout Europe and to various Muslim countries to meet with Muslim and other minority groups as well as politicians, journalists, and anti-discrimination organizations. She is a 2005 graduate of the University of Chicago Law School, where she was staff editor off the* University of Chicago Law Review.

Spiritual evolution works like a standardized test taken on the computer. Every time you get a question right, the computer moves you on to a harder question. But if you get it wrong, it moves you to an easier question. Similarly, if you interpret God's signs correctly, a veil is lifted, and you comprehend God and the purpose of life more clearly. With each "right answer," you see more signs and keep moving to the next level of increased revelation and awareness. Eventually, you encounter reality. The final veil to be lifted is that which covers the face of your beloved in the hereafter.

Although I have a long way to go and many more veils to conquer, the struggles of my life thus far have resulted in at least a few "right answers," evidenced by a spiritual peace previously unimaginable. During some of these struggles, it was less than obvious that I was anywhere near the right answer. Inner turmoil and severe cognitive dissonance—to the point where I felt myself teetering on the precipice between faith and unbelief—convinced me that my inquisitive mind was going to be the end of me.

In the Qur'an, God admonishes us to reflect. Sometimes, reflection brings anguish. It can take us through complex mazes we never really escape until we are ready to move beyond the maze to a greater challenge.

My simultaneous encounter with Muslim extremism and a feminist realization of self is one of the more philosophical mazes I have encountered. I spent my youth enchanted by a relatively warm and fuzzy Islam. In middle school, my enthusiasm and love for my religion made me an unintentional proselytizer. By high school, I was studying comparative religion. When the news vilified Islam, I defended it passionately, writing manifestoes against the manipulative media representations of Islam.

I eventually recognized this concept of Islam was naive. Moving past it required a lot of tumultuous soul-searching. The journey began when I entered college, where I was assaulted by Muslim extremism. Countless pamphlets extoling the virtues of simplistic Wahhabi thinking floated around the university campus. Books outlining this ideology were stacked up in the prayer room, and the fiery Friday sermons embodied the intense anger behind those words.

Some of these books were written for women by men, purporting to discuss Islam's mandates on various women's issues. The books spoke of women only in terms of subjugation. My innocence was ravaged by the descriptions of women as sex slaves; house servants; satanic temptations; and moral, physical, and intellectual inferiors. The books claimed Islam required these roles for women and that any resistance to this destiny was a sign of impiety—ensuring those women were headed to an indescribably horrid hell.

As I read these books, my identity as a woman was, for the first time, clashing with my Muslim identity. It occurred to me that what I wanted as a woman may not fit with what I wanted as a Muslim. The more I researched the matter, the worse the dilemma became. Islam detractors come in many forms, with some more purposefully destructive than others. When I googled "Islam+women," I stumbled across endless scores of Islamic texts quoted out of context, mistranslated, or citing weak *hadith* (sayings of the Prophet). The websites argued that these mangled quotes constituted Islam's view of women. At the time, I believed them. After all, they were quoting prophetic traditions and other religious texts. How could they be anything but Islamic?

The practical effects of this turmoil were many. Representative of them was my struggle with the hijab, which I had always told myself I would start wearing when I began college—a promise to which I stayed true. It was unfortunate that my adoption of the hijab coincided with my naiveté being shattered by extremist rhetoric. The pride I felt when I wore it was often penetrated by the fact that there were other Muslim women who were being forced to wear it to satisfy some male's whim.

For those women, hijab was not a symbol of independence and liberation but precisely the opposite. It held them down, suppressed their individuality, and made them compliant to another's will. And these women were not just abstract figures described in a textbook. I ran into them frequently around school and at social gatherings, where they were almost uniformly timid, slinking back from attention. I knew it was a logical fallacy to equate oppression with hijab—once I adopted it, I wore it for many years, and in subsequent years, I have met hundreds of incredibly inspirational, strong women in hijab. But at that fragile point in my spiritual growth, observing what was around me, I couldn't help but increasingly come to fear that my wearing the hijab helped legitimize its use as a tool of subjugation.

Even worse than the male imposition of the hijab was what I call the Hijab Cult, developed by Muslim women in the community. This group ostracized women who didn't wear hijab, making them feel like lesser Muslims, somehow weaker in their faith than those who wore it. Even though members of this cult were backbiting or constantly judging others' actions according to their personal rubric of proper Islam, they were still elevated as a symbol for all of those "immodest" women to emulate. The hypocrisy was stifling.

Associating the hijab with harshness, I found my relationship with God was becoming primarily based on fear, rather than being properly balanced between love and fear. I worried incessantly about being judged by Him, and it sometimes felt like His disapproval was manifesting itself in the anger I sensed within my community.

Looking back, I see my plight as a necessary struggle. We all have important causes to which we are innately drawn. My cause has always been twofold: women's equality and Islam. For the world to make sense to me, women and men had to be of equal worth and dignity, just as Islam had to be the true religion. Before

I encountered the extremist interpretation of Islam, my world seemed wonderfully whole. Afterwards, my world became fragmented. To glue it back together, I had to reconcile sex equality and Islamic piety.

It took years for me to achieve any semblance of peace, which came largely through long periods of observation and contemplation of what I later discovered to be God's signs. He was initiating dialogue, and through time, I came to embrace that interaction. As I continued to read, I encountered a wide variety of books about spiritual purification and other issues beyond the extremist rhetoric. I questioned the reasons behind my feminist bent. Following hours of meditation and, eventually, greater self-realization, I learned to better distinguish between the environmental and instinctual sources of my ethics. And more importantly, I discovered an Islam that was welcoming—similar to my high school Islam, but far richer and more complex than any Islam I had before encountered. For me, the intricacies of Islamic legal interpretation, the depth of Islamic spirituality, and the breadth of Islam's acceptance of variable practices forever disproved the extremist version.

Whereas before I had always feared subjectivity and variability in religion—mistaking these characteristics as somehow being antithetical to absolute truth—what I learned from my studies of Islamic law and legal interpretation is that subjectivity actually underscores religious authenticity. If Islam, aside from its essential core, is about interpretational diversity—allowing room for people's cultures and personalities to determine what is religiously "right" or "possible" for them—then there is a greater likelihood that Islam is the true religion. After all, truth must be accessible to all, and universal accessibility is impossible with black-and-white interpretations that place most of the world outside the parameters of "proper" Islam. And it was precisely this that I learned of my religion: Islam is, at its core, a religion of dissent. It is not premised on an endless list of do's and don'ts but is instead multifarious and openly accepting of multiplicity.

One of the bases of multiplicity is culture. As Dr. Umar Abd-Allah explains in his article "Islam and the Cultural Imperative," Islam spread throughout the world by adopting the culture of the people it sought to convert. Muslims did not brand these cultures "foreign" and invalidate them in the name of "Islam"; instead, they incorporated everything *except those ideas that clearly contradicted Islamic principles* and used those elements to make Islam acceptable and, eventually, indispensable to the people. Islam spread when Muslims stayed true to all of the Qur'an's fundamental principles, including its message of acceptance.

It was precisely this message that helped heal the rupture between my identities as a woman and a Muslim. My understanding of Islam continues to evolve, but it has finally found a solid foundation. As a woman and an American, I have certain values and inclinations that are, at the core, moral. And I had finally encountered an Islam that embraced this core and encouraged me to use it to do good things for myself and others. In realizing these actions would draw me closer to God, I obliterated yet another barrier between Him and me. It was a momentous victory.

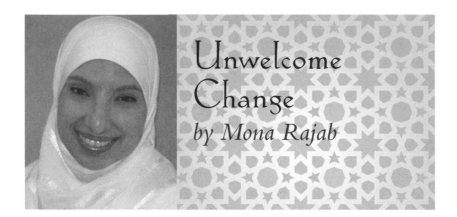

Unwelcome Change
by Mona Rajab

Mona Rajab was born and raised in St. Louis, Missouri. She grad-
uated from the University of Missouri-Columbia with a bachelor of
arts in French and Wichita State University with an MEd in early
childhood special education. In 2009, Mona moved to Damascus,
Syria, with her husband, Issam, and four children, Ayman, Sarrah,
Zayna, and Layla. She currently teaches English at Al-Wataniya,
a Syrian national school. Mona dreams of one day earning a doc-
torate in education and becoming a university professor.

I still remember this scene from a movie I watched about twenty years ago. It showed a teenage girl leaving for school on an
ordinary morning. As soon as she's down the street, she pulls a
miniskirt out of her bag and slips into the bushes to change. Or
perhaps she'd hidden the skirt in her mailbox. I don't remember
now. I recall nothing else about the movie except that one scene,
which has flickered on and off in my mind a thousand times.
Perhaps that is because there was a time in my life when I could
identify with the girl and her secret rebellion. I used to do the
same thing. Only in my case, it wasn't a miniskirt I was hiding.
It was a hijab.

Each morning, I would hide the hijab in my purse. As soon as I closed the garage door, I would sneak it out of my purse and quickly tie it around my head while pulling out of the driveway.

I remember being at the mall once, sporting my new look, when I ran into some family friends who were Muslim. The look they gave me was priceless. It was as though I had grown another head, and they were trying to act like they didn't notice.

I wonder if other Muslim girls have experienced the same strange reactions. A disturbingly large percentage of the people I have encountered (many of them Muslim, unfortunately) makes it seem as though I have chosen to bring my life to an end by wearing hijab. Some even look on me with pity, as if to say, "Poor, backwards girl." Over the years, I've learned to just smile and say to myself, "Whatever."

Although I was born and raised as a Muslim in the US, I can honestly (although shamefully) admit Islam did not play a prominent role in my life until the past ten years. Religion was part of my life to the extent that I acknowledged being Muslim and most of my teachers and peers knew I was Muslim, but it was by no means a priority.

My parents have always been moderately religious. They have both performed *Hajj* (pilgrimmage to Mecca). My father, who has been in this country for nearly half a century, has never missed a single Friday prayer in the mosque. I cannot recall a Ramadan during which he did not read the Qur'an at least twice. As a child of four or five, I remember sitting with him as he taught me the shortest chapters of the Qur'an. Years later, he would occasionally remind me to review these few, brief surahs "so I could teach them to my children in the future," as he put it. That was about the extent of my father's religious directives. From his perspective, he would be happy if I just "stuck to the basics" of Islam—praying, fasting, reading some Qur'an—without going "overboard" and wearing hijab.

To almost all who knew him, my father appeared a fairly religious man, and depending on their own level of devotion, he may have even seemed somewhat strict. This made it all the more difficult for me to fathom why, many years later, he would be so disappointed in me for something I thought would make him proud. I now realize my father's mentality has been embedded in culture, not religion. It's hard to change the mentality of a seventy-seven-year-old man who still thinks hijab is for old ladies—an unnecessary accessory that could only hinder a girl's path to success. This unexplainable contradiction—my father's apparently strict adherence to Islamic rituals and his lax adherence to Islamic principles with his own daughter—remains a thorn in my side. I've tried to make excuses on his behalf. "That's just the way he was raised," I've tried to convince myself over and over again. But at the same time, another part of me would shout, "So what?! It's wrong!"

To my father, I was voluntarily ruining my life. For me, it was a time of spiritual metamorphosis. Had I undergone this transformation in solitude, perhaps the trials and tribulations would have been fewer. What puzzles me, even to this day, is how my closest family members and friends could become my greatest antagonists during my quest to seek the pleasure of God. In my eyes, I was only doing the bare minimum, what I should have been doing all along—dressing more conservatively, attending *halaqas* (study group) increasing my Islamic knowledge. I was atoning for the empty pages in my book of life by making the pleasure of God my utmost priority. To them, however, I had gone too far. I had become "extreme." I became overwhelmed with confusion, disappointment, and at times, loneliness. My own father did not speak to me for weeks.

I still cringe when I remember the looks of disgust he would give me when he saw me leave the house with my head covered, or even worse, wearing a *jilbab* or *abaya*. He would look at me and then turn away, as though the sight was too repulsive to accept. It was as though I had committed some abhorrent, shameful act. Once, as I was leaving the house, he said, "It's going to be hot today." I thought to myself, "Um, yeah, and your point is …?" Instead of being sarcastic, however, I pretended not to hear him. What did he expect—that I would cheerfully say, "Okay," and whip off my hijab? That being half a degree warmer than everyone else would be enough reason for me to change my mind and stop wearing hijab? Why was it such a big issue for him?

I knew why. He never said it, but I knew. He worried I would never get married. He worried I would never get a real job. He worried people would think I was backwards or un-American. It wasn't easy living with these presumptions. I never said anything. I just hoped he would get over it. Now, seven years later, he accepts the fact that it wasn't just a phase I was going through, but something permanent, whether he likes it or not (and I know he does not). Maybe because I'm married now and no longer live with my parents, I don't care as much about my father's negativity toward my hijab—or at least it doesn't affect me as much as it used to.

After much thought, I have come to the conclusion that in my case, the most painful struggles I experienced while growing up in America had little to do with prejudice, discrimination, or peer pressure. Instead, the most poignant conflicts were with family members and friends who mocked my "sudden" approach to religion. I clearly recall the first day I "officially" wore hijab. I was visiting a friend, and a relative of hers commented, "And your mom let you? And you're not even married?" Obviously, this person had grown up in a culture much like my own, where girls don't wear hijab until after they've lured in a husband. I let the comment go, but to this day, her words still get under my skin.

A few days later, my aunt joked in Arabic, "What, you wear hijab now?" I answered in the affirmative. She laughed and said,

"Oh, really?" as if it were a ridiculous idea. One friend accused, "I would have expected it from [so-and-so], but not from you." "Thanks a lot," I thought to myself.

Why was it so hard for everyone to accept that a person can change? Was it because my mother didn't wear hijab and that our family seemed "normal," so I was going against some stupid cultural rule by wearing hijab? Why did my friend make me seem like such a horrible person for choosing something I felt was good for me spiritually?

Other comments were slightly more tactful. At a wedding, a friend of my parents said, "You know, there's a saying that goes, 'If you have something beautiful, you should show it.'" That was one of the more subtle reactions. A later conversation with my uncle, on the other hand, was downright blunt:

"Mona, do you want to know how you can make ten thousand more dollars?" my uncle asked, almost teasingly, one evening. I sensed his attempt at humor, so I started to laugh.

"Wow! How?" I asked excitedly.

"Take off that hijab that's on your head."

He wasn't joking; he was deadly serious. My uncle may as well have smacked me in the face. For a moment, there was silence. I was livid. My face burned with anger as I forced myself to hold my tongue. If it were anyone else, I probably would have just rolled my eyes and walked out of the room, disgusted. Out of respect for the ties of kinship and the fact that I was a guest in his home, however, I remained seated.

He continued, "How much is it worth to you? Ten dollars? Twenty dollars? Thirty dollars?" I'm not sure if he was trying to bribe me to stop wearing hijab or if he was trying to tell me it was worthless. In any case, his sarcasm bothered me. The fact that his voice was becoming increasingly louder almost frightened me.

"I don't put a price on it," I replied quietly, trying my best to appear unshaken by the confrontation. Little did I know this would just be one my uncle's many deliberate stabs at not only my hijab, but my general *deen* (way of life).

I can't help but recall the words of a dear friend. She seemed to be my only support during times of turbulence and strife. When I sought advice about how to deal with my family's response to my wearing hijab, her answer was simple, yet profound.

"Is it more important to please people or to please God?" she asked. Her words remain with me to this day as a constant reminder of my intention in this life, which is not to seek the acceptance of others but to ultimately seek the pleasure and mercy of the Almighty. Yet in my prayers, I still ask God to make my father pleased with me.

The University of Life

by Jameelah Xochitl Medina

Jameelah Xochitl Medina is an educator, business owner, published author, poet, artist, and student. She first began writing poetry at twelve years old and has been drawing since 2001. Jameelah is the author of The Afro-Latin Diaspora: Awakening Ancestral Memory, Avoiding Cultural Amnesia *(2004), designer of a Hijabified 24:31 line (hosted at* cafepress.com*), and owner of* The Medina Academy of Overachievers, *a private tutoring program for all ages. A third-generation Muslim African American, she was born and raised in Southern California as the youngest of six children. Jameelah earned her bachelor's degree in Spanish from Claremont McKenna College and her master's in education and teaching and learning from Claremont Graduate University, where she is currently a PhD candidate. Her research focuses on social justice issues, including Muslim women's experiences with Islamophobia in higher education after 9/11. The White House Project nominated Jameelah for inclusion in* Oprah Magazine's *list of eighty women leaders of the future. She loves to travel the world and has lived and studied abroad in Spain and Panama.*

The best gifts I have been given by God include being born Muslim, being born unto my parents, and being born black in the United States of America. All of the vicious and subtle racism I have dealt with as a black person prepared me for what I have experienced as a Muslim woman in the US after September 2001. I went from being prejudged and mistreated due to my black skin to being hated and stereotyped due to my headscarf. Past and present experiences have helped shape my consciousness as an African American and as a Muslim.

As an African American Muslim, I love my black kin and my Islamic family. As a soul in this world, I love my human family. Members of my families have caused me pain in this life, and the pain is always worse when it comes from those I love and adore intensely. Religion involves a code of ethics, so my expectations of my fellow Muslims are much higher than my expectations of non-Muslims. This is especially true regarding racism, because bigotry contradicts the ideas and values the Prophet Muhammad (peace and blessings upon him) stood for throughout his life. In his last speech on Mount Hira, he strongly admonished against racial superiority and race-based discrimination. Yet too many of my fellow Muslims have abandoned the part of the *sunnah*, the way of the Prophet Muhammad, that has taught us there is no difference between a black person and a white person.

Although the most hurtful experiences I've endured in this life have involved members of my Muslim family, my heart still beats enthusiastically to the drum of Islam. Muslims sometimes test my faith by asking me if I am *really* Muslim (I wear full hijab, mind you). They ask me to recite *Surah al-Fatihah*, the opening chapter of the Qur'an—or they just assume I know nothing of Arabic or the deen.

Four years ago, I was seated on a Royal Air Maroc flight from JFK to Casablanca. I was seated between my sister and a Moroccan woman. The woman asked me, "Are you Muslim?" I responded that I was. At that point, she asked me if I knew the Qur'an. I said, "Yes, I know some." Unsatisfied, she then started reciting the Surah al-Fatihah, prompting me to join her. I went along. When we ended with the word, "*Ameen*," she nodded her head at me in approval. This wasn't the only "test" I've been given. I have twice been asked to recite the *shahada*, the Muslim declaration of faith, before entering a mosque.

Other times, I've overheard Muslims speaking poorly of black people and referring to them as "slaves" in Arabic instead of using the word for "black." When they are confronted about calling black people slaves, they feign colorblindness by pointing out that *'abd* (slave) is also an honorable term used for those who submit to God. Obviously, black people aren't the only ones who submit to the will of God. The "slave" slur is used to identify us in conversation as black people, not to highlight our piety. There is no racial hierarchy in Islam, with Arabs on top and African Americans on the bottom. No race holds a monopoly on the religion.

Although I am thankful for the positive experiences I have had with Muslims, my negative experiences with racism and bigotry are numerous and serve to expose an ill in our community we don't speak about. We can easily point out the ills in other communities and discuss our plight as Muslims in a volatile climate. Nevertheless, as a Muslim "community," we do not talk about racism from within. Many times, we refuse to even acknowledge that racism exists, and when we do have the courage to mention it, nothing is ever done about it—no constructive dialogue, no conferences, no symposiums, nothing.

African American Muslims I know *do* discuss racism in the *ummah*, the Muslim community, because we are living it. When racism in the ummah is mentioned among racially diverse Muslims, too many Muslims run from the conversation or try to disqualify any arguments exposing it.

This needs to change. This has to change. Ignoring a problem does not mean it does not exist or will go away.

It is frustrating and disappointing to catch hell in mainstream society for being Muslim and also within the Muslim community for being African American. When I am not perceived as an oppressed Muslim woman in need of liberation, I am seen as an ignorant and potentially unruly black woman who cannot possibly be true to the din.

Muslims often speak lovingly about the ummah but—may God forgive me—many times, I find myself asking, "What ummah?!" Many days, I live my religious life between a rock and a hard place, but *Alhamdulillah* (praise be to God), I have been heavily blessed with a solid foundation in my own spirituality and have come to understand that—although having one is very nice and comforting—I do not need an ummah to practice my din, live my life submitted to God, or remain committed to achieving the *jannah* (paradise or heaven). Although I sometimes hurt, my beliefs and my faith do not ebb and flow in response to the acceptance or rejection of my co-religionists, *masha'Allah* (God has willed it).

These are lessons I have learned at the School of Hard Knocks or, as my daddy would say, "in the University of Life." My siblings and I grew up as the only blacks in many arenas: ice-skating lessons, swim meets, gymnastics competitions, and our private school classrooms. My parents encouraged self-reflection, contemplation, and discovery as well as choosing companions wisely. With those experiences and my natural introversion, walking the lone and sometimes lonely road is nothing new to me. My family and my few like-minded friends meet my interpersonal interaction needs, and, ultimately, Islam is an intimate relationship one has with God; an audience is not necessary. This worldview helps me successfully navigate within and between my Muslim world and my non-Muslim world. That is not to say there is no struggle within me. All growth requires struggle, and experiencing anger and sadness as a result of being rejected by Muslims was parts of my process.

There came a time, however, when I realized anger harmed my soul and compromised my peace of mind. I realized sadness gave Muslims too much power over me and my mental wellness. With the help of God, the way in which my parents raised me, and my personal disposition, I accepted my life as an African American Muslim as divinely willed, as a test and as a mercy. That does not mean I have resigned myself to racism and racist treatment. It means I know why I live my life and how it should be spent, and part of my time here shall be spent correcting wrongs with my actions, my words, and my thoughts. This is true for racism in the ummah and for Islamophobia in mainstream society.

Navigating between worlds involves code-switching between languages and understandings and requires fluency in binaries. I have been doubly rejected, dually suspected, and persistently subjugated as an African American and a Muslim. Many non-Muslims see my headscarf and the way I dress and automatically assume I am a foreigner with limited English language skills, am passive and docile, or have been abused and forced to cover. This has been made clear during numerous visits to medical centers, government offices, markets, and movie theaters as well as at work and school.

In my professional life as a training consultant, I always find it an adventure to walk into the training room as the facilitator. I can see the cognitive dissonance in the perplexed looks in the participants' eyes, on the deep wrinkles on their foreheads, and in the odd looks and brief whispers. It is always a relief when the shock and novelty of my appearance has worn off and the participants appear more relaxed and behave as if my appearance is irrelevant, which, of course, IT IS.

I was recently on a planning committee for a conference at a university. The chair of the committee and I had been in constant contact via email and phone. When we met in person the morning of the conference, the normally very articulate woman began stumbling over every word. Her eyes blinked rapidly as her brain attempted to connect her preconceived notion of me with the person standing before her. It would have been funny had I not felt so much pity for her at the moment.

Another time, I had to present findings from a yearlong research project before a corporate executive committee. When I entered the room to set up, the committee members' conversation came to a halt, and the room fell deafeningly silent. They sat nervously in their seats, staring at me, unsure what to make of whom they saw. I realized they were so affected by my headscarf that I needed to break the ice, so I incorporated humor into my setup procedure. As they laughed, I saw their bodies relaxing, and I knew they were ready to focus on the presentation. I love being able to make a living doing something I enjoy, with the added benefit of exposing non-Muslim professionals to an educated, articulate, and assertive Muslim woman, which I hope will challenge some of their preconceptions and stereotypes about visibly Muslim women.

In my academic life as a doctoral student, I thoroughly enjoy my learning process, and I am very conscious of my role as a stereotype-breaker in the classroom just by being myself—a self-described nerd. Many times, professors have thanked me for sharing my perspective in class discussions and classmates have expressed appreciation for what they've learned—and unlearned—during our classroom dialogues. We can all adopt the false notion that race and religion do not matter, but just the fact that I receive thanks for my presence and perspective proves otherwise. The fact is that very few people are colorblind or faith-blind, and I have come to realize that the more positive comments I receive from non-Muslims, the more hyperconscious I become of the importance of my religion and my role as an ambassador for Islam.

It is fulfilling to know people are shifting their paradigms because of my presence and contributions in the classroom, but it can also be emotionally and mentally taxing. While trying to overachieve in my professional, academic, and religious worlds, I continue walking on this long, lonely road, with Islam on my right shoulder and African America on my left. Even when I tire of being forced into ambassadorship, I am grateful and realize the blessings bestowed on me. I have plans, and God has plans, and He is the Best of Planners. So while my plan is to go out each day in search of knowledge, righteousness, and economic sufficiency, God has placed me in certain fields, arenas, and circumstances. He plans for me to cross paths with others in search of knowledge. It is a dual blessing, because whenever we teach, we also learn. I was born an African American and Muslim in the United States of America because God knew I could handle the tasks along both journeys.

I love being an African American *Muslimah*, a female believer. Masha'Allah! I derive strength and consciousness from both of these aspects of my being, and I would not have it any other way.

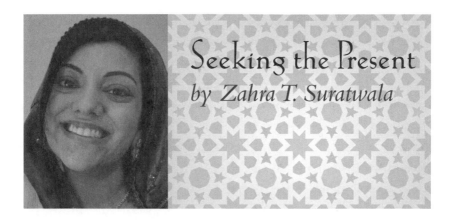

Seeking the Present
by Zahra T. Suratwala

As President and CEO of Zahra Ink, Zahra T. Suratwala writes, edits, and serves as a marketing consultant for a variety of small businesses. She has found a way to combine her love of writing with her desire to pursue projects that can truly affect change—the result is a small business she takes very seriously and finds intensely fulfilling. Zahra obtained her master of arts degree in English literature from Loyola University in 2003. She has lived in Egypt and Thailand but will always call Chicago home; she loves its beauty and its fickle weather. When she is not writing, Zahra can be found causing a ruckus with her husband, son, and daughter. If home is where the heart is, her home is firmly placed in their hands.

I have led an uncomplicated life. In this essay, you won't read of major obstacles or character-testing trials. I have not been tormented in the search for myself or my place in life. I have had solid relationships with my parents and my religion. I enjoy the acceptance of my community and my peers.

And yet. There has been a sense of not-quite-contentment that has trailed me since college. Feelings of nostalgia for where I have been—or longing for where I am headed—that have not allowed me to be fully present for each stage of my adult life.

College was a four-year whirlwind during which I found people who made me feel comfortable just being myself. They were like family. I was nestled in a bubble from which I didn't care to emerge; my life was idyllic and I had it all. As graduation loomed near, I already found myself anticipating my next great adventure—moving to Cairo, Egypt. I planned for and anticipated Egypt so much that when I got there, I wondered, did I fast-forward through senior year a little too quickly? Nostalgia hit me, and that wouldn't be the last time.

Egypt was a grand experience during which I became fully independent. I found I could conquer—and conquer I did. I saw more of the world on my own than ever before, I gained peace and immeasurable blessings through *ziyarat* (pilgrimage) to the Al-Hussein mosque in Cairo, a site revered by both Shi'is and Sunnis, named in honor of the Prophet's grandson, the Imam Hussein.

Yet even while I was in Egypt, I looked forward, as always. I anticipated the day I would fall in love and get married. I thought about the future and what it would bring. Alongside this anticipation was nostalgia for the Egypt experience; I began to miss it before I had even left. I found it extremely difficult to stop looking back or looking forward and to simply be in the moment—to enjoy my remaining time in Egypt and to actually move on when the time came.

During the next few years, I fell in love and got married and obtained my master's in English literature—and still, I missed Egypt. My husband, Taher, and I moved to Thailand after our wedding. Only when we returned to Chicago and I felt a new nostalgia for Thailand did I miss Egypt less. I had replaced one longing for another.

See a pattern? I was rooted in the past or dreaming of the future, but in the present I had rarely been. I feel as though my adult life, Alhamdulillah, has been a series of wonderful stages or adventures. And yet in the midst of them, even as I knew I was experiencing something that was changing my entire world, I could not avoid looking forward and backward. I could not help but continue to see my life as a series.

All along, I knew something in my life would have to change for me to change. It turned out that something was a small, beautiful blessing we call Yusuf: our son. Yusuf supplies the ultimate perspective. He reminds me I have so much to be thankful for, including a lot of experiences that preceded motherhood. I am thankful for college; it helped me bloom. I am thankful for Egypt; it fortified me and expanded my capabilities. I am thankful for Thailand; it gave me a year of newlywedded bliss in which to settle into my marriage and create memories that are ours alone. Now, however, I do not wish to be back in any of the earlier stages of my life. I have conquered my habit of looking back.

Learning not to wish myself forward, however—I am still learning how to do that.

I look at Yusuf and imagine him being in the next stage. When he was still tiny and colicky, I prayed for time to pass more quickly so we could leave colic behind. Before he learned to smile, I so wanted to see his face break into a grin. Now that he is smiling, even laughing, I want to see him sit up on his own. Next month, I will want him to crawl. I don't want to miss out on the precious moments I have with him now because I am too eagerly looking forward to the next stage. If I keep looking ahead, I will not fully experience or appreciate where he is now. With Yusuf, I see more clearly than ever before, how much I do this forward-looking. Yusuf can be the catalyst I need to finally stop looking to the future—and to live in the present.

Yusuf has been more than a spotlight on this nagging habit of mine; he has also been a reminder of what is, for me, the meaning of life. Living in the moment means recognizing this unique, fleeting chance to make the most of the opportunities I have. Yes, this includes the opportunity to enjoy my son as he grows—he will never be this small again, he will never need me this much again, he will never be so continuously by my side ever again.

Yet it also means the opportunity to sow that which I want to reap after my life here is over, to do the work it will take to find salvation. Two and a half years into my marriage, I embarked on the spiritual journey of a lifetime: the hajj. I wanted to go early in life so I could begin the rest of my life having been changed by Hajj. I expected the experience to be moving and inspirational, but I did not expect it to penetrate so deeply. After Hajj, I vowed to live up to this experience for the rest of my life—to meet the responsibility of having understood what is the right way to live and to behave and knowing precisely how to achieve this rightness.

I know the only way to honor this vow is to recognize my blessings. To be the kind of Muslim I want to be—one who adopts God's rules to the extent that they become second nature—I have to stop here, in the present, and recognize I have all the opportunity in the world to become that person. I am blessed with a life free of conflict, with a religion that will lead me to truth and peace, with a husband and son and family that brings me joy and loves me.

On another level, I have to also recognize that someone very young and brand-new looks up to me and will continue to do so as he grows older. My son will learn about life from me, and knowing this, I find myself hoping the culture and religion upon which I place so much value can be instilled in my child. I am a place where cultures meet: America meets India meets Islam. I am many things. And above all, I am a Muslim. I find myself needing to articulate my relationship with my faith so I can pass on my perspective of it to my son. My notions of womanhood and motherhood are informed by the inextricably linked planes of my religion, my nationality, and my gender. I hope they serve me well as I take on a duty that will last my entire lifetime.

And so. Whether I slow down and enjoy myself, appreciate my life and take advantage of my opportunities, or I fast-forward through it all and spend my time wishing I were a few steps ahead or behind where I am—either way, I will one day arrive at the end of my life. And at that point, I will see how important it really was to savor the journey. The only way to get what I want out of this life, to end up where I want to end up, and to achieve the right result is to make the most of each day right now. I want to live each day for what it is, with all of the strength and beauty my religion infuses in me. I want to live for today, for that is truly living.

Author's Note: Since this essay was written, we have welcomed a second child to our family: our beautiful daughter, Nooriya.

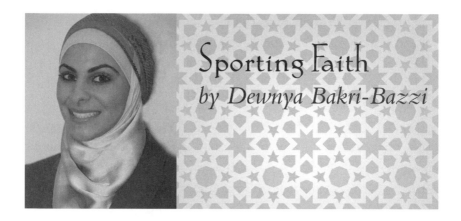

Sporting Faith
by Dewnya Bakri-Bazzi

Dewnya Bakri-Bazzi attends Thomas M. Cooley Law School in Michigan. She received a bachelor's degree in political science and criminal justice from the University of Michigan-Dearborn, where she also played basketball. Although Dewnya was born and raised in Dearborn, Michigan, she remains deeply attached to her roots in Jnoub, South Lebanon.

"You cannot play in the tournament because your uniform does not conform to the rest of your team's uniform."

I was raised to be a God-loving individual, a person who under no circumstances should replace the Almighty as my number one priority. I would have never imagined this quality would become my biggest obstacle to participating in normal, everyday events in this free country of America.

Along with my strong religious beliefs comes the personal decision to maintain a conservative lifestyle. On a daily basis, I wear a scarf on my head, long-sleeved shirts up to my wrists, and full pants to my ankles. This includes my basketball uniform. I was eight years old when I first put on a scarf, and even though many coaches, referees, teammates, and even fans had a problem with it, I would not change my decision for the world.

Playing sports while wearing hijab is not a distraction or limitation as some may assume. When I played in tournaments and at other schools, however, it was a difficult task to make them understand the concept of the hijab. Many spectators refused to accept it. I would be stared at and talked about, but through it all, I never once thought to myself, "Maybe I should not have put a scarf on; maybe others are right, and it was not worth it." Instead, I took their negative attitudes as motivation. At the end of the day, it did not matter what I was wearing if I proved myself on the court. A good performance would in turn gain their respect. So every time I put on my Nikes, I knew I had something to prove. I knew I could not have too many off nights because each one represented a little respect lost—not only for me but for my religion. I was not only representing myself; I was also representing my faith.

My passion for basketball carried through to my college days at the University of Michigan, where I was a shooting guard for two years. The lack of respect for my uniform that I had experienced from fellow citizens, students, and teammates during the previous twelve years continued and even worsened in college. The coaches became less accepting, the referees became tougher, and the crowd became more hostile.

Although the uniform I had been wearing for several years had been approved by the district board of athletics and the NAIA (National Association of Intercollegiate Athletics), I was forbidden by referees to play several games during my college career because of it. This helped me realize two things: 1) while I am being held back because of my religious beliefs, I must not be the only person who is experiencing this; and 2) although our constitution separates church from state and the courts recognize this difference, there are people out there who do not.

"Why do you wear that scarf?"

"Doesn't it choke you?"

"Are you able to perform with it on?"

To my critics, my silent (and sometimes verbalized) answer was always, "Yes, I can! I can perform, and I will perform." I tried to be humble. I tried to address the critics in a way that was neither arrogant nor aggressive. Yet they continued with their outrageous questions.

"Can you hear?"

"Can you see?"

"Doesn't it affect your peripheral vision?"

Then came the holy month of Ramadan. Many critics thought I was going to die because I would not eat or drink while taking part in conditioning drills. My teammates, however, were amazed. They asked questions and thought I was so strong for being able to handle the workload with no food or water. Some of them even tried to fast for a day to see how it was. It was rewarding to see them trying to understand the concepts and to realize they respected my perseverance.

When I first joined my college team, my teammates thought Islam was a religion that preached violence, killing, and terrorism. Now, one year after my departure from the team, many of my former teammates are curious about Islam. They saw how I carried myself, were impressed by my disposition, and realized that if I represented Islam the way I did, it had to be a great religion. Peace, unity, kindness, helpfulness, and gratitude—all were virtues I talked about and tried to embody in my actions on and off the court. Through sheer action, I was able to change their minds about Islam and make them understand what our Prophet taught us.

I found both comfort and solidarity in helping a Christian teammate who believed she could only wear skirts based on her interpretation of the Bible. When dealing with the situation, she came to me for courage and asked me to enlighten her on how to get her dress code approved. I told her the steps she would have to take, and she is now playing basketball in a skirt. Even though this is not the same story as mine, she used me as a role model and a stepping stone to carry out her beliefs. My story is not unique. Every person tries to make their faith fit in with their everyday life.

I want to continue to make a difference. I want to help people. I want people to think, "Dewnya stood for what she believed in, and she succeeded." I want to help pass a far-reaching statute for all levels of sport and other daily activities that allows people to continue in their pursuits without thinking to themselves, "Do I need to change myself in order to…?"

Over the years, I have grown to become what I believe is a good student, athlete, activist, person, and, most importantly, a follower of the truth. This experience has brought me to where I am today. By becoming a lawyer, I hope to help the Muslim community in several ways. One of my objectives is to advise Muslim business owners about how to operate their companies in ethical ways. Since September 11, 2001, the United States government has implemented several laws to prevent money laundering, terrorist funding, and similar activities. These laws, whether we like it or not, focus on the Muslim community. By undertaking ethical tactics and law-abiding policies within orga- nized structures, we as a community can help discredit the bad reputation the government and media have tried to attach to the Muslim community.

All of my life, I have faced controversy due to my religious beliefs. Inspired by my love of sports and sense of personal obli- gation to help others, I have never wavered in my aspirations to follow through with my goals and morals. The constant struggle to do what I love while concentrating on my beliefs was not easy. Many people may look at my story and feel it was not that big of a struggle, that I was playing sports the same as many other students do every day. My struggle was in dealing with those who believed a girl covered from head to toe could not and should not be a part of the world of sports.

When I was in the eighth grade, my athletic director and coach, Mr. Picanon, told me something that fueled my ambition for the rest of my life: "Dewnya, you made history! First hijabi Female Athlete of the Year, first hijabi to earn your varsity letter in all four sports. You are truly an inspiration."

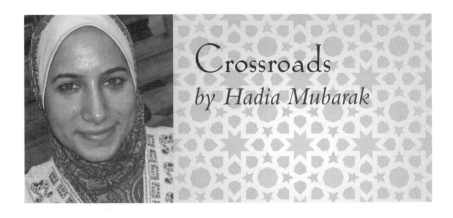

Crossroads
by Hadia Mubarak

Hadia Mubarak is a fourth-year doctoral student in Islamic studies at Georgetown University. Her research interests include classical Qur'anic exegesis, family law, Islamic legal reform, and gender issues in Islam. Mubarak previously worked as a senior researcher at the Center for Muslim-Christian Understanding at Georgetown University, researcher at the Gallup Organization's Center for Muslim Studies, and researcher for American University's Islam in the Age of Globalization project. In 2004, Mubarak was the first female to be elected president of the Muslim Students Association (MSA) National since its establishment in 1963. She earned her bachelor's degree in international affairs and English from Florida State University. Mubarak received her master's degree in contemporary Arab studies with a concentration in women and gender from Georgetown University. A washingtonpost.com On Faith panelist, Mubarak writes regularly on issues of gender, religion, and politics facing Muslim Americans.

I am a product of two cultures, with a tongue that is bilingual and a belief that is universal. My roots belong somewhere in the vast Atlantic Ocean, linking the world my parents left behind with the world in which I arrived. I am lost in the waves that bring me closer to both shores, swimming underneath the ocean's undercurrents in a perpetual struggle to find my identity. My search for this evasive identity seems neverending, stretching beyond the horizons of the sky, the stars, the galaxies, and the microscopic atomic particles that compose our existence.

"Which do you like more, Jordan or America?" sounds as familiar to my ears as the crashing of waves on Panama City Beach or the echoing of the *adhan*, the call to prayer, from the minarets of Jordan's mosques. According to Arab custom—in which children take on the nationality of their father—I am not Jordanian but Syrian. In America, I am neither Jordanian nor Syrian, for tradition rules that you belong to the soil that testifies to your birth and childhood.

This country has witnessed my birth, shaped my perceptions, and socialized my behavior. She knows me as well as I know myself, for my memories evoke her history and my dreams live in her future. I capture her history by writing my own. I sleep in her nest of security, my fears soothed by her magical lullabies. She is the needle that holds my thread, interweaving my story into her all-encompassing quilt. I have fallen in love with her way of life, her personal freedom, her respect for individuality, and her cultivation of diversity and tolerance. I embody her defiant characteristics. Her First Amendment writes the letters I stamp and mail to my congresspersons; signs the anti-war, anti-apartheid, anti-occupation, and civil rights petitions; protests in front of the Capitol during rain or shine; and vocalizes my moral outrage. My appreciation for these ideals is reinforced by my religion, Islam. Inspiring a belief in one God and in humanity's ultimate accountability before the Creator, Islam has been central to shaping my identity as an American.

What does it mean to be an American Muslim? The concept of an American Muslim has eluded American public consciousness. In the post-9/11 climate, American Muslims were confronted by a sense of perpetual displacement in the American public psyche. Although we had been born and raised in this country and knew no other place to call home, I and other American Muslims came to realize for the first time that we were not perceived as American in the eyes of a large swath of the general public. As our religious beliefs became a reason for our incrimination after 9/11, as our organizations and places of worship became the target of vandalism and hate crimes, and as we were perceived as potential threats to the security of our own nation, we felt our very identity as Americans was being subjected to scrutiny, challenge, and contestation.

The struggle to legitimize our identity as American Muslims existed long before 9/11, however. At Rutherford High School, I was nicknamed "Arabian Princess," "Camel Jock," and "Magic Muslim" by my classmates. Although generally curious and understanding, they defined me through the prism of my faith and ethnicity. They saw my foreignness before they accepted me as an American. I was the girl who stood out, who never really belonged. My knowledge of global events and the US's self-interested role in the Middle East challenged their perceptions of our country as a beacon of goodwill in the world. My classmates often resisted my attempts to offer a glimpse of a world they had never seen—except through clips of beheadings and headlines that screamed terrorism. For some, the media confirmed their perception of me as not being "really American."

Still, I reached for the upper limits of success, becoming editor-in-chief of my high school paper, playing soccer, running cross country and track, creating the ISLAM (Interested Students Learning About Muslims) Club, and achieving a class ranking of fourth out of 385 students. It was only through those endeavors that my ethnicity and religion ceased being my defining characteristics to my teachers and classmates. With the passing of time, I eventually became the student journalist, the soccer player, the Honor Roll student, the classmate, and the friend. My true friends, however, never had to make that transition from respected tolerance to a comfortable normality. From the first instance we met, they saw a human being, not my religious or ethnic identity.

The constant need to validate my identity continued beyond my adolescence. I recall an uncomfortable experience while applying for a campus job as an undergraduate student. I handed the receptionist my social security card, a blue rectangle with nine ink-smudged digits, as a required form of identification. The receptionist told me she needed my passport as well. Surprised, I questioned the necessity of a passport. She then called in her supervisor, who had been the one to request my passport in the first place.

"Aren't you an international student?" she asked.

"No, I'm not," I clarified. "I'm an American citizen. I was born in New Jersey."

Her mouth dropped. She stammered, "Oh, you're not?"

I do not have to wonder what it would feel like to be treated as a foreigner in my own county, to never really belong, to be a ragtag hanging on the periphery of American culture. I live that reality daily. The cloth I wear on my head is mistaken for an attempt to cling to a foreign cultural tradition paired with a reluctance to assimilate. Ironically, hijab is still not fully accepted in my parents' culture. A statement of my belief in God, the hijab I wear has nothing to do with culture.

In college, I was shopping for steak at the local deli one day. The kind old man standing next to me started making casual conversation about steaks.

"So where are you from, India?" he suddenly blurted out.

"I was born in New Jersey but raised in Panama City, Florida," I responded. "My parents are from Jordan and Syria."

With a look of surprise, he inquired, "Why do you still wear that traditional clothing if you're living in America?"

Looking down at my jean skirt and gray Calvin Klein shirt, I knew he was referring to the scarf on my head, the piece of cloth that often erects barriers and evokes deeply embedded perceptions that are difficult to overcome.

"This is not cultural," I said and pointed to the scarf. Had it been cultural, perhaps my friends and relatives overseas would cover their hair as well. Perhaps I wouldn't have been the only girl in my entire summer school in Jordan to cover her hair. A belief and commitment to God transcends all cultures. Faith is not derived from culture or the city in which one is born. Faith is a product of one life's experiences, fears, hopes, and the realization that one's ultimate fate rests entirely in the hands of a higher power. Faith breaks down barriers. It does not create them.

People assume someone is forcing me to wear hijab, and I feel insulted every time. Anyone who knows a single thing about me—my parents especially—know I could never be forced to do something in which I did not believe. If I did not believe in what the hijab does for me as a woman, I'd have absolutely no motive to dress as I do. I relish the freedom the hijab gives me, the freedom from having my body judged on a scale of 1 to 10 by strange guys who mean nothing to me. I have no desire to participate in an unspoken, undeclared beauty pageant, one that increasingly teaches young women their value is based on their physical appeal rather than their talent, personality, and intelligence. The hijab gives me a sense of empowerment, allowing me to decide who sees my hair and my body—and when they can see it.

When others view my hijab as a failure to assimilate, I am reminded of the obstacles that lie ahead as I struggle to validate my roots as a Muslim Arab American, molding the missing piece of a puzzle that can bridge those worlds. I began to realize many people do not see me but rather an image they have formulated in their minds from glimpses of Hollywood movies showing Arab fanatics hijacking a plane or from a *Dateline* documentary about female honor killings or some book they've read about a Saudi Arabian princess escaping the oppression of a male-dominated society. Before they've even learned my name or seen me kick a soccer ball or debate an argument, they have judged me and think they know who I am.

An identity neither begins nor ends on a stretch of land, for an identity lives within the heart and the consciousness. Land erodes, land evolves; it is plundered, and it is cultivated. It is not the master of its destiny. An identity is elusive; it can be neither contained nor defined by standards other than its own. Encompassing, defiant, and alive, the American Muslim identity is that of the ocean, its waves washing over diverse shores and merging their remnants into one entity.

Secularizing My Graduation
by Arshiya Saiyed

Arshiya Saiyed is a Teach for America corps member in Nashville, Tennessee, where she teaches ninth-grade English. She recently graduated from Centre College with a bachelor's in history and government. Arshiya is passionate about democratic politics, closing the achievement gap, and discovering new, delicious recipes. She was born in Chicago, Illinois, but she was raised in and currently calls Shelbyville, Kentucky, home.

Growing up in Shelbyville, Kentucky, offered a predictably normal existence: attending Friday night football games, skipping morning class to get McDonald's, and spending lunch gossiping with my girlfriends. I, however, represented a well-known yet rarely discussed difference. For me, there was no Sunday morning Bible study, I had never been saved during a Fellowship of Christian Athletes club meeting, nor did I feign interest in the passion of Christ. My knowledge of American law, religious injustice, and even some aspects of my own faith—especially those regarding its mainstream image—I learned in seventh-grade World History, ninth-grade Civics, or twelfth-grade AP Political Science, not a in a madrasa or terrorist training camp.

That is precisely why my opposition to graduation prayer during my senior year in high school was born out of rationale rather than zealousness. The perception of my faith, however, obscured my secular intentions and spawned a media frenzy, a Christian community movement, a KKK protest, and the one event that made me an outsider after nearly a lifetime of fitting in.

Engel v. Vitale, Lemon v. Kurtzman, Lee v. Weisman: I cited them all during the second Senior Class Committee meeting as we discussed graduation arrangements. Having recently studied these in government class, I felt exceptionally smug as I turned the discussion from caps and robes to the laws of our country. It just wasn't constitutional for the principal to choose a student to lead a prayer, I told a group of mostly evangelical Caucasian Christians and our class sponsor, a teacher who had probably never heard of the Supreme Court striking down prayer in public schools. I was not alone in my fight to secularize graduation. The movement had been born through other students, mostly from my AP Politics class. Students from all faiths and political persuasions acknowledged the injustice of graduation prayer at our high school, and our small minority decided to work to change it. Recognizing I could claim the most discomfort from the actual prayer, I became their leader.

But our words were lost on the Senior Class Committee, and I found myself in one of the most uncomfortable situations I could imagine. The classroom grew hotter, and I felt myself shrinking smaller as my classmates accused me of breaking tradition, picking a fight, or simply trying to gain attention. The other students who supported the secular cause were also belittled. They were harshly silenced, while the backlash centered on me. The opposition's comments grew more personal and outrageous. The pressure continued to intensify, characterized by an insult free-for-all and witnessed by those who sympathized (including my old friends and certain school administrators). When the meeting was finally over, I left the room, fighting back tears. I stayed composed long enough to find an empty classroom. There, I literally fell to the ground and struggled to breathe while I cried and simultaneously prayed to God to protect me.

I knew my intense rush of emotion and my feelings of not-belonging were not unique. Two years before, my sister had graduated from Shelby County High School as well. She threw her cap into the air above her hijab, just moments after the principal-chosen student—soon to join the ministry after a well-known born-again experience—expressed the need for non-Christians to either find Jesus before they die or burn in the fires of Hell forever. As convincing and fruitful as that may have seemed to the student-minister, I didn't want to hear it on my special day and knew I was legally protected against it.

My faith played very little role in my decision to pursue what I believed was my constitutional right to reject proselytizing prayer in a state-sponsored setting. Indeed, I rejected compromises offering to hold an Islamic prayer in conjunction with traditional Christian or nondenominational prayer. It was just as unlawful and unfair for me to force others to hear the words of Islam and pressure them to accept God on their graduation day as it was to force me to listen to others' prayers. Shelby County High School obviously did not understand the concept of nondenominational prayer, as this broad definition was used to justify the proselytizing and evangelical prayers of years past.

I stuck to my Supreme Court precedents and arguments regarding separation of church and state, but the matter had grown much larger than I imagined. My Muslim identity kept me focused on pursuing what was right and just, but the situation became perceived as a conflict between Islam and the traditional values of a small Southern town.

By the end of the third Senior Class Committee meeting, I had been verbally harassed by students and teachers alike; I had lost the majority of people I considered friends; my pleas with the principal had gone unheard; and my use of the laws of our land—not those of my faith—had been ignored. It was the first time in seventeen years I had genuinely felt like an outsider in my home. My Islamic faith became the one factor that made me innately un-American in the eyes of my former friends and community.

After a strongly worded letter from the American Civil Liberties Union, several harassment complaints, and consideration by the Shelby County School Board attorneys, the situation grew beyond the boundaries of my school. It became a struggle of church and state and a question of Islam's ability to assimilate into an American context. The numerous other non-Muslim students, teachers, and community members who shared my secular arguments were ignored in the media's portrayal of a young Muslim girl's *jihad* (struggle) against the practices of her community and country.

I was featured on international terrorist watch blogs, written about for months in the local newspaper, prayed for during a large Christian community gathering, and even marched against by the local Ku Klux Klan (KKK). I became the personification of a community's frustration and discomfort with inevitable change. The blogs and KKK portrayed me as a young rogue jihadi-communist bent on destroying the freedoms of America, while my town made me into an enemy with the goal of secularizing all things holy. Even some Islamic community blogs picked up my story and bluntly called me a bad Muslim with a worthless cause because I didn't cover my hair or demand an Islamic prayer.

The logic of these people escaped me, and I felt alone and without a team to champion me in a time when I was losing faith in myself. I began to question my own motives and wondered why I had chosen such a difficult task when I could have quietly sat through an offensive graduation. But I recognized that what I was fighting for was a fundamental right, and no amount of harassment and dissuasion would change the laws that upheld my crusade.

The battle to secularize my graduation was about more than just me. It was a difficult adventure that ignited a community, highlighted minute religious differences, and became an emotional journey for everyone involved. Eventually, the school chose to avoid legal action and not hold a prayer at my graduation. I walked across a heavily police-controlled graduation stage with an American flag, watched by my supportive family, news cameras, and booing members of the crowd. Above my head, a plane appeared with a banner reading "Let us Pray." With my diploma in one hand, I extended my other hand to the principal who had worked so hard to silence me.

I could have easily been silenced, perhaps most effectively by myself. The uncertainty of the results, ridicule by my friends and neighbors, and an overall sense of not belonging weighed down on me. I could have stayed silent through my class meetings and even my graduation. I could have allowed the injustice to occur. My graduation day would have been sullied by a few minutes of hurtful and discriminatory remarks—but I knew they did not have to be, so I acted. My family's ideals and my religion's doctrine taught me not to blind myself to those things that were innately wrong. Even more importantly, I had a little sister who would have to suffer through graduation in a few years if I did not stand up for both of us. There would continue to be students who would lack the courage to defend themselves against the actions of the majority.

My diploma was my proof that I was a product of the American public school system, the institution that had given me the tools to protest the graduation prayer. It would be inaccurate to say I had won any kind of religious or moral battle that day. Designed to protect the minority, the great American system had been lost on closed minds. Acceptance of inevitable change had been rejected by closed hearts, and my faith in unconditional community and friendships had greatly diminished.

There was not a moment I did not question my own intentions. I struggled to attend school every morning and face those who had hurt me. I often wondered whether the graduation prayer was worth the sacrifices. Despite these uncertainties, what was not lost and what I will never lose is my belief in the justice and protection of God, my love for American law and the institutions that continue to protect me, and my recognition of the seeds of change and diversity that were planted in a small Southern town.

It has been almost three years since that first meeting where I spoke up against my fellow students and eventually changed the religious climate of Shelbyville. Even now, as a college junior, I am reminded of my experiences. I receive curious questions from fellow students, supportive words from strangers who recognize me, and angry reactions by those who are still bitter and feel I have taken something fundamental and precious from them. I had hoped these individuals would learn respect for the laws of our country and acceptance of diversity. Sadly, these lessons may never be learned by some.

Although I was pressured and mistreated, I've learned no one can ever take another's fundamental and precious faith. This beautiful gift lives inside of us, and public display does not make it any stronger. Indeed, my harsh community brightened my faith, and I am confident saying I did the same for theirs.

As I grow older and gain more perspective on the events of my past, I find it was I who learned the greatest lesson from this trial. My Islam and my family are all I need to carry me through the experience of nearly everyone and everything turning against me. With faith and support, I can conquer future challenges that will test me even further.

A Headscarf Away from Television
by Mariam Sobh

Mariam Sobh is the founder and editor-in-chief of Hijabtrendz. com—*the original fashion, beauty, and entertainment blog for Muslim women. Her journalism career includes working for a variety of media outlets as a news anchor, political reporter, and traffic editor. Although her roots are in Boulder, Colorado, where she was born, Mariam also spent time in Virginia, Saudi Arabia, and Illinois while growing up. She currently resides in Chicago, where she divides her time between work, family, and waiting for her big break.*

Can a Muslim woman who wears hijab actually be capable of reporting the news on television—in America? I always thought the answer was a strong and resounding YES! Because I *was* that Muslim woman wearing hijab, and I was going to do it. I was going to break the barrier and get out there and pursue my dream.

That was me in college. My mind was set. I was completely focused. I finished my master's in broadcast journalism and worked in radio and for the university television station during both undergraduate and graduate school. On paper, I seemed bound for broadcast success. I had internships in radio and television in town. I was even the commencement speaker at our graduation ceremony. People raved about my work and patted me on the back. Nothing ever made me feel I could not make it in my field.

Yet once in a while, a nagging voice in the back of my mind would make me feel self-conscious about my hijab. One of my classmates had once asked me, "What will you do if you don't get hired because of your headscarf?" I confidently responded, "Sue them!" Then a tiny seed of doubt would enter my head, *What if I really don't get a job because of my hijab?*

I started to realize not all was going as planned when I began applying for jobs in television. I scoured dozens of openings across the United States. Every time I sent someone my resumé and demo tape, there was no response. But I kept going. I heard how some graduates had sent out thirty or more tapes before getting their first job, so I knew I had to be persistent.

The first sign anyone had even looked at my work was when I got an email from a station in Springfield, Illinois, about an hour from my home in Urbana. The news director wrote to me and said she thought my tape was great, but that I wasn't what they were looking for. "Keep knocking on those doors," she wrote to me.

Okay, so she didn't care for me. She thought I didn't "have enough experience." That seemed fair, since I was a recent grad. So it was a surprise to me when, a few days later, I saw a former classmate reporting from that same Springfield station. This was difficult to swallow. She was the same girl who had always needed my help, and here she was reporting for a station that had told me I lacked the experience. It hit me. I didn't know the right people. Maybe the rumors about "It's who you know, not what you know" were true.

That little nagging voice of self-doubt grew a bit louder. Could it really be my hijab? No one had outright said it was because I covered my hair. I told myself I just had to give it time. I continued to send tapes and resumés; fifty tapes later, I received a phone call from a news director in Negaunee, Michigan.

"Do you have a job yet?" the news director asked me. I was literally speechless. I told him that I'd love to come out for an interview. They couldn't pay for my transportation but would put me up in a motel for the night, so I drove eight hours to get there despite the winter weather and a severe cold with laryngitis.

The news director used to work for CNN but had decided to settle down in a small town so he could write novels in his spare time. He looked over my demo tape with me and said he was impressed with my work.

"Frankly, I thought you were a lot older. You sound so mature." Inside, I was jumping up and down. Could this be my big break?

The staff at the station was nice and friendly. I felt they saw me as a professional and not as a woman wearing hijab. I was told the job offered only $17,000 a year with no benefits, but that didn't deter me. I needed a job, and I decided I needed *this* job. The news director put me through a screen test. I read the teleprompter as they taped me over someone else's demo tape. I felt bad about that; but at the same time, I thought it meant they were really interested in me.

I was given a tour of the town and taken to lunch. I could feel my dream getting closer and closer and closer. Oddly, the news director never asked me about my skills or my professional experience. Instead, he wanted to know if I had a boyfriend, what holidays I celebrated, and if I could really survive the cold weather. Maybe this was my opportunity to prove just how *American* I was: "We celebrate all holidays, I don't have a boyfriend, and I'm from Colorado, so winter means nothing to me."

"I'll give you a call at the end of the week and let you know what we decide."

The phone call came, and I was devastated. "I think you're too good for this place. You need to go to a bigger town. You wouldn't like the winter here, anyway."

I felt like I was having an out-of-body experience. Was I really hearing this?

I started thinking he must have just wanted to see me in person for his own curiosity.

My self-esteem took a huge hit. Was it my skills, or was it my scarf? I doubted whether anyone would ever tell me it was my scarf, but at the same time, no one was mentioning anything about my skills, either. This was the beginning of what would be many similar experiences in which I would be asked personal questions that had nothing to do with the job being offered.

I found myself pondering my situation. Since television has expanded in the past decade, we now see all kinds of people on the air: skinny, plump, homely, beautiful, and ethnically diverse. There is still, however, a lack of representation for anyone who happens to wear their religious identity openly.

Certainly, I understand the argument that you can't show your religious affiliation on television because people might start thinking you're biased a certain way. My response to this argument is, isn't it better to know someone's background up front? Doesn't reflecting one's religious identity mean we'll hold those journalists up to a higher standard because they must ensure their work doesn't reflect any personal bias? Knowing my religious identity, don't you think I would hold myself to a higher standard? Furthermore, why the assumption that wearing a headscarf means I want to report on religious issues? I'm perfectly content reporting on education, entertainment, health, and environmental stories.

In my naiveté, I had believed in "the American system," only to start noticing through my own experiences that parts of it were reserved for those who fit into the mold. And I knew deep inside that if I took my scarf off, I'd be welcomed with open arms.

Although I had tormented myself through dozens of fruitless attempts at landing in front of the camera, I decided out of sheer determination to give it another shot. I'd been working in

Chicago for a few years and realized that if I didn't do this now, I would never know what my chances of achieving my dream would be.

I hired a professional to shoot my audition tape. I began applying all over the country and never heard back. The videographer told me to be patient. Then he suggested I take my scarf off to get the job and put it back on when I landed it. I felt a little queasy when I heard that.

I approached three television news agents in Chicago. Two of them said they couldn't help me because they didn't think I'd get hired with a scarf. One of them actually gave me an inkling of hope; that is, until he talked to his boss. "Um, yeah, we're actually not taking on any new clients right now. We're just focusing on the talent we have." Then he admitted he'd jumped the gun, and his boss told him no one would give me a second thought.

Feeling down, I tried out for a reality show with a certain celebrity on a whim. I was surprised when they called me back and asked me to come out to LA. That was the spark that led me to start trying out all sorts of avenues to gain exposure. Some people were interested in the novelty of a "hijabi," while others told me I didn't have a chance.

I called the news director in Negaunee, Michigan—the only one who had actually given me a chance to get really close to my dream. I called him because I wanted to know firsthand *why* he didn't hire me four years earlier. He remembered me right away but couldn't remember why he didn't hire me. He offered to look at my tape again but couldn't promise anything. I told him of my struggles and how I knew my scarf was an issue, but if someone was willing to give me a chance, I would not disappoint. He said part of the problem was that at the time of my interview, the climate was so anti-Muslim. He went on to admit that he was embarrassed by the attitude of his fellow countrymen. I didn't get a job, but at least I got some closure.

I have since decided to put my efforts into getting involved in all forms of media. I'm a blogger and podcaster. If no one will put me on television, I can make my own television shows. Why should I let my skills go to waste?

Despite my decision to take my career in other directions, I still feel confident I will eventually realize my dream. I cannot help it. It is who I am. I know deep inside this is the route I'm meant to take in life. The news executive who told me I would never have a chance as long as I wear a scarf doesn't know how stubborn and determined I am. Whether I make my debut as a broadcast news anchor, a television talk show host, or even a bit part actress, there is an opportunity out there somewhere for a strong independent woman who happens to wear a headscarf. I am patient.

In my pursuit, I have learned that happiness wears many scarves. My success is first defined in my goodness as a human being; my identity is not defined by career alone. I have a beautiful daughter, a loving and supportive husband, and a job that has taught me a lot about who I am and my capabilities.

Even if I don't become the first hijabi television news reporter in America, perhaps the pursuit of such a dream has helped open the door for future hijabis. Perhaps that reporting role I dreamt of in college will someday be filled by my own daughter.

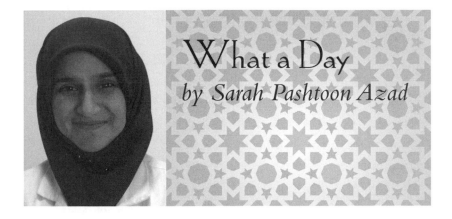

What a Day
by Sarah Pashtoon Azad

Sarah Pashtoon Azad is an obstetrician and gynecologist in the San Francisco Bay Area. She is also a committed youth group leader, inspiring young American Muslim women to lead confident, articulate lives dignified by Islam. Sarah takes an active interest in cultural sensitivity training for health care providers of Muslim patients. In her free time, she's an avid reader and runner. Sarah is working on learning her fifth language.

    5:00. Snooze.
    5:15. Snooze.
    5:30. Snooze.
    5:45. Snooze.
    6:00. Snooze.
    6:15. Snooze.

What? 6:30?! Crap, I'm late for work.

Starting my usual early morning routine, I jumped out of bed, washed my face, threw on my scrubs, and was in the car by 6:35. Then I ran back into the house, grabbed my white coat, cell phone, and purse, and by 6:37, I was on the road. I read my morning litany in the car as I raced to work. This early in the morning, there were rarely cops around, and at eighty mph, I could generally get to the nurses' station in twelve minutes. If only I wasn't supposed to have been there at 6:15. Really, I thought, I've got to start getting more than four hours of sleep at night. How did Malcolm X do it? Nearing the end of my third year of an Ob/Gyn residency, I found these early morning struggles with my alarm clock were getting old.

As I walked into the hospital, I smiled, knowing I was just that much closer to my sister's visit. She was coming that night with her husband and my niece. The past year and a half since my father died had been the hardest of my life. It wasn't the three to four hours of sleep I got every night, it wasn't the eighty-hour work weeks, it wasn't the eight days a month I was on call and had a twenty-six- to thirty-hour shift. It was the loneliness.

When I transferred my residency back home at the end of my first year, I had done so to be with my father during the last few months of his life. It was a whirlwind. Between working, packing, moving, unpacking, and spending time with my father, I didn't have time to think about the fact that I would soon be alone in our family home.

Our family home. That in itself was a problem. Every time I walked past our huge living room, I remembered our family Christmas celebrations, the big plastic tree, the gifts, the warmth. I remembered the parties with the live Afghan musicians and their speakers, the dancing, the police knocking on our door at midnight and asking my parents to turn it down a bit. Every corner of our house reminded me of something.

Suddenly, within three weeks of my father's death, my sister returned to LA, my brother went back to Cal Poly, and my step-mother quit her job and began spending most of the week with her mother, who was suffering from end-stage Parkinson's. I went from a houseful of people to a house that held just me.

During this period, I spent three nights a week out with friends and two nights at the hospital. I would study at coffee shops so when I came home to my big, empty house, I could just finish studying what I needed for the next day of work and fall asleep.

When my sister visited—you know you're blessed when your sister, mother to a small child, comes every month to visit you, wash your dishes, talk with you a few minutes a day, and just be an extra body in the house—I would count down the days. And today was the day she was coming. I just had to get through work. Then I had to remember to order food and pick it up, and then get to the airport. I was so excited.

After work rounds, we went to the board. That day, I was in charge of Labor and Delivery. I'd grown comfortable in the role and although there was a lot of medical management and direction of junior residents, I found it mostly involved managing the chaos that takes place in a busy public hospital.

By 4 p.m., I had finished my last cesarean for the day. As I started rounding, Dr. Smith urgently called me into a room. The patient had had a prior cesarean and was now attempting a natural delivery. As I walked in, the fetal pulse was low. Dr. Smith told me, "Sarah, this is a stat, this is you and me, we'll do this calmly, and we'll do it now." This is what we were trained for, to focus in the face of any medical emergency. I forgot the list of things running through my mind, and I focused.

I calmly explained to the patient (in Spanish) that she needed surgery now and that it was best for the baby. We rushed her to the OR and discovered the fetal pulse was back up, so we let the nurses get her ready as we hurriedly scrubbed in.

We flew through the cesarean. Once inside, we found the baby was already in the abdomen. The old scar on the uterus had ruptured. I quickly pulled him out and passed him off to the pediatricians. Within seven minutes of coming into the OR, the baby was safe. We paused to orient ourselves and then proceeded with the surgery. There was a lot of damage from the uterine rupture and the mother's abdomen was full of blood. We got to work, clamping, cutting, and sewing. We quickly realized there was no way to salvage the uterus and proceeded to remove it.

This is one of the hardest surgeries in our field. The technical skill and surgical speed required demand the best hands. My excitement at being able to do this procedure was hard to contain. Yet that excitement was tempered by the gravity of the situation; the only time we do "exciting" things in surgery is when someone might die. Usually someone with a brand-new baby—a sobering thought.

An hour and a half later, we were done. The uterus was out, and the bleeding had stopped. The stress of saving this patient's life had kept our minds off the other problem: we had delivered a blue baby. Once the surgery was over, a nurse walked in with the umbilical cord gases: 6.81 and 6.83. Any number below 7 indicated permanent brain damage.

I went into obstetrics to care for women and their pregnancies, to save lives, and to improve their quality because God sanctified life—all life. But in the obstetrics part of my job, it was not just about saving the baby from death but also saving it from brain damage. The 6.81 and 6.83 readings were by far the worst I'd ever seen outside of a textbook. But I would have to think about that later. We had to get the mother to the ICU.

Once we reached the ICU, the anesthesiologist got the mother settled, and I grabbed her chart to document this disaster of a delivery. Dr. Smith was waiting. She said, "Sarah, before you do the paperwork, let's debrief." We discussed every step and every moment of the case.

Dr. Smith's assessment: "Sarah, we should have just crashed her. We lost time washing our hands. It probably wouldn't have changed the outcome, but we would both sleep better if we had just splashed the Betadine and crashed her." Four minutes wasted. Mainly to scrub.

Maybe, just maybe, if I had spared those four minutes, I could have saved this baby a lifetime of brain damage. Maybe. I finished up the paperwork, then paused and took two minutes to think. Looking down at my feet and my bloodstained scrubs, I thought about the nature of our job. In this contemporary world with our advanced medical technology, it is no longer just about saving lives. Sometimes, even after working years to perfect our skill and improve our speed, we are able to preserve a life but not its quality. It's the ultimate threshold of our field. Some blame it on the limits of technology. I share the view of those who believe there are some things you just have to leave to God.

The more we accomplish in medicine, the more people expect perfection, and the less they understand it's not always guaranteed. Pregnancy—which was once a dangerous time in a woman's life—has become routine. People now expect perfect babies and perfect outcomes. Many don't understand that God doesn't promise anyone a life without trial. How am I now to explain to a mother that her baby may be developmentally or physically disabled for his entire life? How?

I looked up at the clock: 7:30. My sister! I rushed out of the ICU, postponing my meditation on modern medical dilemmas. I ordered takeout, found the chief resident on call to tell her about the patient in the ICU, changed my bloody scrubs, and raced out the door.

I called my sister after she landed and let her know I'd be a little late. Like a heavenly angel sent to care for me, she said, "No worries, Sarah, the baby is sleeping. We both have books, so take your time. We can sit here for two hours if you need them." Fortunately, I wasn't that late.

As we were driving home, my sister asked, "Did you have a rough day? You're kind of quiet."

"No, we just had a huge complication at the end of the day."

"Oh! Oh! Tell me about it!"

This wasn't out of line for my family, as I often came home with incredible stories about eleven-pound babies, ruptured ectopic pregnancies, or crazy gynecologic surgical cases. But I was really not in the mood. "You know, sometimes at my job, when things go wrong, people get hurt." We drove home in silence.

People talk about "not bringing work home," but how relevant is that to me? How do I ignore the fact that we made a decision this afternoon that was sound but in hindsight may have caused a life of developmental disability? While I get to play with my perfectly healthy niece? How do I ignore it and just enjoy my evening so I can have some sense of normality in my life? Maybe doctors aren't allowed normal lives. After all, God doesn't guarantee anyone a perfect life.

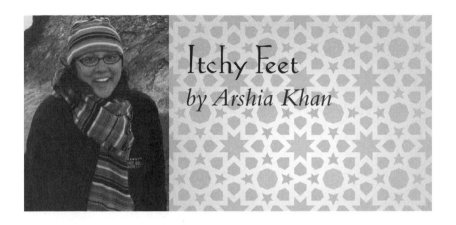

Itchy Feet
by Arshia Khan

Arshia Khan currently lives and works in Khartoum, Sudan, where she is a program officer with the United Nations World Food Programme. She holds a master of arts in International Studies from American University in Washington, DC, and a master of arts in natural resource management and sustainable development from the UN's University for Peace in Costa Rica. Arshia has interned in Chile; served as a Peace Corps volunteer for environmental conservation in Malawi, East Africa; and hitchhiked and backpacked across Southeast Asia, Latin America, and southern and eastern Africa. She is an avid outdoorswoman who aims to climb the highest of mountains and spend as much time as possible enjoying the splendors of nature. A dedicated environmentalist, Arshia wishes to combine this passion with humanitarian issues and poverty alleviation. She strongly believes environmental harmony is at the foundation of peace and prosperity.

As I was growing up, my favorite magazine was *National Geographic*. Even before I could understand the articles, I was captivated by the brilliant imagery and stunning photography.

My imagination ran wild, my eyes eagerly seeking depictions of the exotic. Unfamiliar animals, vast forests, mighty rivers, towering mountains, and people who dressed and painted themselves like nobody I had ever seen before—my mind was continually dwelling on an adventure and wandering the globe as I soaked up these images.

One day, when I was around four years old, I watched a television commercial I still remember vividly today. The advertisement itself was not particularly colorful, but because it was so moving to me, that moment stands out as one of my first vibrant memories. It was a Peace Corps commercial, a two-minute piece that enchanted me for a lifetime. At that moment, I realized that I, too, could go to those places in the magazines and I, too, could live an adventure. My feet began to itch, and my dreams to see the world through travel and exploration began to take shape.

My reality was quite different. Growing up in the white suburban Midwest, living in a town surrounded by non-Muslims, and lacking people of color other than my own family, I learned being a Muslim girl was difficult. Added to that was my lust for exploration and resistance to norms. I was a tomboy who grew up preferring to ride dirt bikes in the woods with my brother over playing house with my sister. My secret pastime of stargazing involved climbing out the window onto the roof of our house.

My first reaction to the social limitations of an adolescent Muslim girl was one of rebellion. It had not occurred to me that the restrictions placed on me as I grew older came from my parents' commitment to Islam and love for me—not out of sheer malice as I pretended to believe. Unfortunately, my narrow religious teachings had only included rituals, not theology. Thoughtless recitation of verses in a foreign tongue seemed dogmatic to me because I understood none of the implications of my recitals. The motions lacked spirituality and were reduced to unbending tradition. This is not my parents' fault. They, like most

Pakistanis, had been raised with a cultural emphasis on religion. Only in recent years have they realized there is more to religion than simply going through the customs, and this has enabled us all to see the real beauty of Islam.

When it came time to choosing colleges, I felt enormously restricted. My first desire was to study marine biology, but I was informed that good Muslim girls do not wear wetsuits, and so, after many fits of frustration, I changed my major to environmental science. My new choice was not entirely supported, either; anything related to the environment was a new field for Muslims, most of whom choose the established occupations of business or medicine. What could a Muslim woman possibly have to offer to the world of environmental professionals?

I began to realize if I was going to persuade my parents there was nothing wrong with my choice, I needed to convince them of Islam's approval. I must be honest and say I initially just wanted them to stop badgering me. As I read more about Islam's connection to the environment, however, I recognized its importance and began to appreciate the depth of my religion.

One of the most moving verses I came across was also the shortest: "Assuredly the creation Of the heavens And the earth Is a greater [matter] Than the creation of men: Yet most men understand not." (40:57.) The grand schemes people have built over the millennia and pay homage to pale in comparison to the wonders of God, yet nature is so often dismissed as passive scenery. I also read the Prophet Muhammad (peace and blessings upon him) had spoken against the destruction of trees and had taught that animals also pray to God and, having souls, must be treated with reverence.

I then understood that what I had seen as only a passion was actually a calling and that after all of the rituals and sacraments, my religion had a profundity that could not be harnessed through mere movements. I came to understand that even though there are strict regimens and doctrines that everyone must adhere to, no two practices are alike, and the interpretation of what is important in each person's Islam is as individual as the person herself is.

With this discovery, I returned to the decision I had made nearly twenty years earlier: I would join the Peace Corps. Knowing my parents were still not as enthusiastic about my revelations as I was, I brought up the decision to join delicately. I knew my parents' opposition to the idea, the inevitability of an impassioned and bitter debate, and my inability to handle the disappointment of their refusal.

In the end, I emptied my heart into a letter and hoped. I explained my desire to see the world and help people in whatever capacity I could while protecting our environment. It was hard for them, but through my lifestyle, they were forced to recognize that just because a woman is unmarried, it does not mean she cannot take care of herself and do amazing things. While I never did receive their permission to join the Peace Corps per se, they did recognize my necessity to do it. And so I packed my bags for Africa. I was now becoming the *National Geographic* explorer I had always dreamed of being.

Except it turned out to be much different. One thing I learned is pictures are glossy. Even ones depicting famine, carnage, and sheer misery—all are smoothed over by the luxury of not being there, not having those eyes look back into your own, not having to inhale the fumes of disease and sickness, not having to hear the wails of desolation and despair. Seeing a mere image will never do justice to bearing testament with your own eyes. Yet it would be false to paint a picture portraying everyone in Malawi as leading a wretched life; on the contrary, the most beautiful smiles and joyous laughs I have had the pleasure of beholding are Malawian.

My assignment in Malawi was to live in a remote village on the fringes of protected areas and help the residents become more conscientious of the need for conservation, while simultaneously increasing the standards of living. It was a tall order. I departed for my village as a representative of the United States. When I arrived, my new neighbors noticed I was not exactly what they expected—I was neither white nor male.

To most rural Malawians, differentiations among races were limited to black or white. No other race existed. They knew I was not exactly white, and I certainly was not black, so they were very curious about my background. I had not anticipated the need to announce my ethnic or religious heritage, but perceiving their inquisitiveness, I began to open up. I spoke about my family being from Pakistan, their immigration to the US over thirty years ago, and our Islamic faith.

It was fascinating to see their reactions. This was early 2002, and conversations about September 11, 2001 were still relatively fresh. Many people wondered aloud how I could possibly be both a US citizen and a Muslim, with parents from Pakistan no less—where the most wanted man in the world was supposedly hiding. I explained things had gotten ugly in the aftermath of the atrocities, but many Americans are becoming educated about US foreign policy and are moving away from accepting Muslim stereotypes.

My village had no prejudices against me based upon my faith; they were simply amazed at my multitude of attachments. They were not ignorant about Islam, either. Nearly 20 percent of the population practices Islam, making it the second-most prominent religion in Malawi. Many uninformed Westerners view the developing world, especially Africa, as being a place of violence, primitiveness, and intolerance. Yet it was those same uninformed Westerners living in the US, the "freest" society on earth, who had harassed my loved ones for wearing hijab. People in Malawi are open-minded and do not concern themselves with which religion you practice, so long as you have faith in a being greater than yourself.

What they had difficulty accepting was that I was a woman alone in Malawi. When I arrived in the village, my coworkers were disappointed to learn I was not a man. My religion was of no concern, a mere curiosity and conversation starter, but my gender led them to believe I would not be able to fulfill my roles and duties as a volunteer. It was very discouraging—to have fought all of my life against sexist prejudices, only to find them in the very place where I thought I would be emancipated.

After realizing most officials with whom I was assigned would not take me seriously, I struck out on my own and met other villagers, who gave me a chance. They saw me living amongst them in a thatch-roofed home lacking electricity and running water, far away from anyone I had ever known, and they knew I was doing this for them. As they saw me cook local foods with fire on my mud stove, drag a hoe through my kitchen garden, and balance a bucket of water on my head, they realized I was trying to understand what it meant to live their lives, what it meant to be Malawian. And so they also knew I was there for myself as well.

As I worked among these wonderful people, people with such strength and sensitivity, I realized I was not wrong in my choices. I wish I had not been as headstrong when confronting my parents, yet I believe they understand at a deeper level that my Islam may be different from theirs but not subordinate.

Religious interpretations are as myriad as the stars; each person on this planet represents a unique way to practice his or her religion. What makes Islam so wonderful is it means something different to each and every one of the people who are brought together by it. Islam is unity through peace and diversity; it is not conformity or blind submission.

Being in Malawi taught me faith in oneself is just as important as faith in God, and recognition of others for their goodness is just as essential as respecting them for their piousness. I do not practice the daily habits of Islam as my parents do. Nevertheless, I am still a Muslim woman who loves her religion and is proud to declare it. The days are passing in which the only sign of devoutness is through showing your face at events; rather, what is in the heart is where true faith lies. One of the great pillars of Islam is the paying of *zakat*, or charity. *Zakat* is not an obligation of the rich and able; it is the right of the poor. To me, it should not be thought of as an annual donation, but rather, a lifestyle reflecting your heart. That is what my Islam means to me.

After completing my Peace Corps service, I traveled for six months in Africa before returning to the US for graduate school. Now that I have finished my studies, I hope to revisit Africa and continue my work in sustainable development—my living *zakat*. This time, I will not veil my heritage or discuss it only when asked. I will wear it as a badge of which I am very proud.

Being a Pakistani American Muslim woman working in foreign aid means my uniqueness brings fresh ideas and perspective. Just because there are not many of my demographic in the field does not mean I should return to a traditional lifestyle. Even though I have this long label attached to my persona, in the end, I'm still me: a woman with her own thoughts, ideas, and passions. I am a Pakistani American Muslim woman, but I am not one who will be bound. I have itchy feet; why would anyone ever want to stifle that?

Moment of Truth

by Ruqayya Raheem Gibson

Ruqayya Raheem Gibson advocates for the emotional development and empowerment of families and youth. She has worked in non-profit management for several years, writing grants that have raised over $1 million to fund programs for families affected by Hurricane Katrina. Ruqayya also produces independent documentary films with an emphasis on social justice, vulnerable populations, and self-esteem. Her awards include the American Mental Health Alliance (AMHA) Community Leadership Award and the Association of Black Social Workers (ABSW) Community Advocate Award.

I have always known God was in control of everything in our world, but there were times growing up when I doubted if I was one of his favored. My mother converted to Islam in the seventies, and we were among the only members of my large extended family who were not Christian. As a child, I grew up ashamed: ashamed of my name, ashamed of my religion, and ashamed of my lack of material possessions.

I was raised in the inner city of Chicago, where most of my friends and family had names like Esha, Monique, Dameon, and

Robert. My name, however, is a strong Arabic name: Ruqayya. I love the power and meaning in that name now, but as a child, I pretended it wasn't mine. Children teased me, calling me "African bootie scratcher" and "dirty African" because of my name and my religion. The people I grew up around were Christian and celebrated Christmas and Easter. For years, I was teased for not having Christmas presents, until I realized that since my birthday was so close to Christmas, I could pretend my birthday gifts were actually Christmas gifts.

Despite these challenges, I understood that even if the outside world made me uncomfortable because of my religion, my extended family always made me feel right at home. There were even times when Granny and Aunt Julia opened their homes to my family so we could have a place to sleep during times of transition.

My mother eventually got a good job and moved my brothers and me out of the hood and into the suburbs. Even after moving away, I was haunted by memories of nights sleeping in a crowded bed in a crowded house.

I had witnessed a lot of things—things a young Muslim girl shouldn't see. I watched family members sip Crown Royal like it was iced tea, observed drug interventions performed in the living room, rode down Ashland Avenue on late nights searching for my runaway cousin, and saw my first crush get shot down in front of his house.

I had seen so much, but I was also given jewels of faith. My father was a devoted Muslim who never missed a prayer. My mother was a calm faithful woman who always said, "We plan, and Allah plans—who do you think is the best of planners?" I was taught that no matter what was going on around me, I would be victorious as long as I was obedient to God's will. I was taught that God gave me experiences in life to prepare me for my moment of truth. I had faith that I had a purpose and the hard times

I had experienced were for a reason, but up to this point, I had been unable to figure out what that reason was.

My moment of truth came on August 29, 2005.

Hurricane Katrina hit a city not too far from my home in Houston. I was devastated by the stories I heard about families being separated from one another. I watched the news footage of human beings trapped for days on rooftops, in the Superdome, and in the convention center. I wanted to do something. I knew God was in control of all things in this world and that for some reason He had allowed this atrocity to happen. I prayed to Him, asking Him for guidance on how I could assist these people. I stayed glued to the television as survivors arrived at the George R. Brown Convention Center. I wanted to go out and help, but I knew I was only one person.

Then I remembered the Prophet Muhammad (peace and blessings upon him) was just one person who'd had the guidance of God. I knew if I allowed God to guide me, even little ole me could make a difference. My mother and I loaded my sons into the car and headed to ACTION CDC, where we took phone calls from survivors and people looking for family members. It was frightening at first, driving to strange apartments; taking food, money, and clothes to families all over town; not knowing if people would accept what you gave them or forcefully take everything you had. Every time hesitation crept into my mind, I would think about how I would feel if my children and I were suddenly in need of a helping hand in a new city. I kept volunteering day after day, week after week, and month after month. I focused on the people and the lives in limbo. I saw images of my own family members as I looked into each person's eyes, and I had faith that somehow we were all connected and I was doing what God wanted me to do.

The families we helped also helped me. I, too, felt more complete. I felt as though I had been prepared to help make a difference in the lives of survivors for whom God had allowed hardship to occur. I felt as though everything I experienced in my youth had trained me for my work in Katrina recovery. I turned this powerful volunteer experience into a career. I knew this was my calling and my purpose, and with the help of God, I have been able to secure over $1 million in funding to help more than 6,000 survivors reclaim their lives.

The trials I experienced as a girl equipped me to relate to people who are struggling to start their lives over. Seeing my family struggle instilled empathy in my heart, teaching me to care enough about others to stand up and actually do something. Had it not been for my firsthand witnessing of domestic violence, drug abuse, and poverty in my own family, I would not have been able to say to the survivors, "I know you can make it through this. Just have faith" and *truly* mean it.

One day, I looked up and realized three years had passed since I had begun volunteering in Katrina relief work. My children had grown. They had accomplished and learned so much—and I had missed many moments of their lives. I wished I could get the time back, but I couldn't. I felt guilty for a moment, but then I was reminded I had been called to do this work and my work was not done yet. I had many more lives to touch, with God's permission. I had met so many people whom I'd attempted to help. Ultimately, it was these resilient individuals who had helped me.

One special woman has stayed in my heart and mind through these years. Her name is Glenda Carter, and I feel deep down that God wanted me to meet her. Glenda was a courageous sister who survived Katrina, only to be told she was dying of cancer and had eight to twelve months to live. She lived every day of her last year with joy and respect for life. With all that she was enduring, she still found the strength to help others in need, even allowing friends who had lost their homes to stay at her house, never expecting anything in return.

Glenda was always smiling and exploring new ways to help her six children enjoy every moment they shared together. I visited her in the hospital several times and during each visit, with tubes in her nose and needles in her arm, she smiled effortlessly. Glenda told me, "You're either gonna make it through the storm, or you're gonna drift off in it, and I'm gonna make it. Don't worry about that 'eight months to a year.' Nobody has that say but God."

I was humbled by her strength as she stood on the brink of uncertainty. I had helped so many people over the past three years, but I couldn't help her. I could help get her bills paid and offer a kind word, but in the broad scheme of things, nothing really compared to giving her more years with her beautiful children.

The world should hear about the Glenda Carters of the world, who do everything they can to help their family recover while life moves on around them. Glenda reminded me how important it is to cherish every day of my life, accomplishing good in this world by caring for my family, helping the needy, and always being submissive to God's will. My children know Glenda's story and realize her children no longer have their mommy. My children are already learning about empathy and faith.

I now understand the suffering I experienced as a child had prepared me for my newfound purpose: helping those in need. I have the knowledge and awareness to protect my children from witnessing the more brutal parts of life. As they each begin their own journey in search of their purpose, I hope they will embrace every aspect of who they are. I know now that God made me who I am for a reason, and I would not change any of the things I was ashamed of as a child.

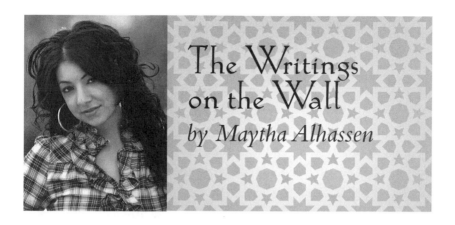

The Writings on the Wall
by Maytha Alhassen

Maytha Alhassen has dedicated herself to bridging her worlds of community organizing, social justice activism, academic research, and artistic expression. She earned a bachelor of arts in political science and Arabic and Islamic studies from UCLA as well as a master's in anthropology from Columbia University. Maytha is currently a doctoral student in American studies and ethnicity at the University of Southern California, where she works as a program assistant in the Middle Eastern Studies Program. While at Columbia, she conducted research for the Malcolm X Project and worked with arts-based social justice organization Blackout Arts Collective. As a member of the collective, Maytha facilitated creative literacy workshops with incarcerated youth at Rikers Island, helped organize the Hip Hop Film Festival at the prison's high school, and wrote an introduction for One Mic, an anthology of the students' art and poetry. Maytha also works as a performer and organizer for play productions of Hijabi Monologues, *co-hosts Arab-American–themed TV variety show* What's Happening, *and writes for the blog* Kabobfest. *She has participated as a member of the Arab Complete Count Committee of Los Angeles and was the Los Angeles coordinator of the Arab Film Festival.*

Verily He Who ordained the Qur'an for you, will bring you back to the Place of Return. Say: My Lord knows best who it is that brings true guidance, and who is in manifest error.

—SURAT AL-QASAS, 28:85[1]

In certain Arab Muslim cultures, travelers write this verse from Surat al-Qasas on a wall of their home before departing on a trip. This ritual is practiced to ensure the safe return of the traveler. This was the case in my home: regardless of the distance, every single time we took a flight anywhere, my mother insisted my five siblings and I all adhere to this tradition, even those who had not yet learned to write (for them, she held their hands over the pencil as she wrote out the five-line verse).

This visual image stands out for me as a ritual part of my life—and one I refused to practice during the period in my life when I overtly disavowed my Islam. My conscious outward objection reflected the inward wrestling of faith I had been experiencing as I entered college—a year before 9/11.

It was in post-9/11 New York—a space and place still crippled by the attacks, so clearly framed in terms of "Muslim fundamentalism"—that I rediscovered Islam. I was not looking for a counterculture rebellion banner to wave, nor was I recruited to bring down the "immoral West." I did not pack political beliefs in my knapsack as I journeyed on this road of self-discovery through winding, circuitous religious trails. In a time of loneliness, 3,000 miles away from my family, I felt a void and turned to my desire for God-consciousness as my spiritual compass. And, in the midst of the journey, I found the beauty and spirituality of Islam through signs in the heavens, in Malcolm X's diaries, in the eyes and words of believers, and from the writing on the wall. As a traveler, I had to return home to know where my future would take me.

---

[1] Abdullah Yusuf Ali, *The Meaning of the Holy Qur'an* (Beltsville, Maryland: Amana Publications, 2002).

In college, even before 9/11, I had begun straying from Islam, not necessarily in my actions or intentions but more in my identity. As "one of them"—someone America considered "suspect" based on religious or ethno-nationalist identifications—I could go in one of three directions: hold onto my religious beliefs and operate under the radar; take a strong, almost militant affirmation of my religious or nationalist identity; or engage in an all-out assault on my own identity. The problem is I embody two of the sectors America most fears: I am Arab *and* Muslim. In America, this combination is not a unique phenomenon, but it definitely represents a minority.

On the day the towers were struck, my father adopted the under-the-radar approach. I told him he had nothing to worry about with regards to me because, "I don't look Arab. Everybody here thinks I am Mexican." I thought to myself, "I'm lucky no one thinks I look Arab." In the middle of that thought, I experienced a dramatic shift: "Lucky?! I should not have to hide my Arabness! Who cares what anyone thinks about me. I am ARAB!"

It was at that moment that I affirmed my ethno-nationalist identity with real conviction. Yet even as I rediscovered my Arab identity, I turned my back on Islam, hoping the shadow of religion would fade away as I ascended an Arab hill. Dismissing the traditional practices of both my nuclear and extended family, I protested against Islam in an effort to make sense of my post-9/11 identity in a college environment. I alienated myself from my family, separating from them not only physically but in a more profound, spiritual sense as well.

I stopped praying; refused to fast during Ramadan (the first time since I had begun the practice in fourth grade, never having missed a day); avoided Islamic functions and Muslim-dominant spaces; and refused to cover my head as we recited chapters from the Qur'an during visits to my grandmother's grave. In an act of cultural rebellion, I stopped writing the eighty-fifth verse of Surat al-Qasas on my wall before traveling. It was important for me to communicate to my parents, family, and society very clearly where I stood, lest they be confused about my belief system. I was no believer. My outward resistance, I insisted, had to be articulated cogently in an explicit, unambiguous rejection of religious practices.

As this transition took place, I found myself in an environment more culturally diverse than my high school setting. I was introduced to multifarious ideas and cultures that were actually tolerant of the Arabness I had grown accustomed to hiding. Yet even with this tolerance, I adopted an either/or attitude towards the construction of my identity.

Religion was visibly under attack in the elitist circles of the ivory tower. The Western philosophy of Sartre, Nietzsche, and Feuerbach functioned as my sword of choice as I attacked monotheistic, Abrahamic religious traditions. I tried to forge modern science into a shield, a bulletproof armor to protect me from invasive religious thoughts. I vehemently believed a path of scientific existentialism was the only way to understand my vulnerable human condition. I wavered back and forth between labels, even calling myself an agnostic or an atheist at different times. I considered joining the Atheist Association of America before adding yet another identifier into the mix: "Cultural Muslim."

I imagined I had a new understanding of "God." I laughed at the way my family and relatives surrendered to and worshiped what I envisioned as a Greek god of days gone by. I asked myself, how could they believe in and turn to a God who created the universe, when science had all the explanations and required a much more rigorous process for proving truth?

I didn't understand then that *I* didn't understand the complexity of belief, faith, and the ideational complexion of God. I was the intellectual plebian, assuming this "God" was to most believers an anthropomorphic Godhead fixed in the billowy clouds of the heavens that they bowed their heads to in prayer and worship.

I underestimated people's spiritual and intellectual depth while at the same time overestimating my own intellectual aptitude.

During this phase of skepticism, I critically analyzed religion, phenomenology, metaphysics, and anything that appeared to have a tinge of what academia likes to categorize as "pseudo-science." I now know this phase was necessary for me to arrive at what Ibn Arabi calls "double vision." It was then, alone and far from my family, that I opened myself up to explore my heart's pain, begotten from separation. And it was then, with an accepting heart, that I was open enough to see the signs I received. My school and work projects became points of intersection centering around Islam, unconsciously stirred in that direction. The internal and external positioning of this verse spoke volumes to me: "We put our signs into the horizons and into ourselves" (41:35). Malcolm X said, "Allah always gives you signs, when you are with Him, that He is with you."

Around this time, my master's thesis led me to begin meeting with Arab students on campus. These gatherings eventually turned into a series of Muslim talks and events all over the city of New York.

My intent was clear: "I am exploring my Arab identity, not Islam. Islam had its chance to save me from persecution when I was a child. What could it possibly do for me now—after 9/11?" In my attempt to swim upstream, to wade back to shore, the currents continued to pull me this way and that—always back towards Islam. Why? I thought I was done with it—I thought I had cut it out of my life and placed it in a box of school photos and track medals, hidden away nostalgia. Islam was not finished with me, however. I had never really allowed myself to freely swim in its waters.

I came to understand this "current" more coherently during a visit home from NYC, when I unintentionally pulled back the plush velvet drapes a little too far and saw the writing on the wall. I traced my fingers over my mother's familiar Arabic script. I couldn't get this image out of my head or the surge of emotion out of my heart. Even though I didn't believe, my mother still did—both for me and in me.

A few years back, I was asked to contribute a piece exploring my perception of God for an interfaith art exhibit organized by a fellow Muslim student at Columbia University. (This was, as it became clear later, yet another testament to the abundance of God's signs.) What, to me, best represented God? What did God mean in my life? Thinking about this haunting image, this writing on the wall and my years of religious wandering, the notion of faith in a safe return home emerged. For the artwork, I took an overexposed photograph of the vertically striped wallpaper smeared with Arabic pencil marks. After developing the picture, I painted "al-Qasas" in Arabic script across the photograph.

After I explained to visitors the story behind the artwork, an interesting reaction emerged. In the responses of other people, strangers even, I understood something about myself that had been beyond my consciousness at the moment I was producing the piece of artwork. The significance of that moment and stroke of the paintbrush cannot be overemphasized or understood deeply enough. In that moment, I felt I reclaimed my Islam. Although I had started identifying myself as Muslim again, this was the first time I had felt it. It was a completely new perception: the statement was turning inward and planting its seedling in the gardens of my soul. My mother, back in Southern California, was not present to see the final version of the piece or its placement in the exhibit. I had written Surat al-Qasas back on the wall and into my life.

Not only did this verse—used as a supplication to bring a safe return from travel—literally bring me back home to West Covina, California, but it also metaphorically "returned" me to my religious point of departure—and ultimately to my spiritual destination, to my creator.

O Soul made peaceful
Return to your Lord accepted and accepting
—SURAT AL-FAJR, 89:27–28[2]

As I retell the story of my relationship to Islam, I feel strange speaking of "going back." This somehow misrepresents the nature of my journey with faith. How can I "go back" if I never truly left? In retrospect, my bouts with questioning God's existence were part of my understanding of faith. My faith was strengthened by the depths of doubt and disbelief excavated from this world's soil, where I discovered "hidden treasures that love to be known." As Ibn Arabi says, God is not just "being" or "existence," but something that must be found.

I had to understand "there is no god" to fully apprehend the simple complexity of the testimony of faith, the profession that "There is no god but God, and Muhammad is his messenger." There was no "god" because this was the "god" Nietzsche had proclaimed "dead," the one Feuerbach had argued was man "self-alienated," and the one Sartre had claimed stifled a human's progress towards creating his or her essence, because this "god" is human-made, a societal "god." Living my life by the rule of this human-made, societal god had led to my dissatisfaction with religion and my overall unhappiness.

In retrospect, I realized I had to live fully in that space of disbelief in "god" to lay the foundation for authentically accepting and preparing my soul to receive the true God. The profession of faith, which stands as the first pillar of Islam, radically asserts, "There is no 'god,' but God, and Muhammad is his messenger." Such a simple phrase took me a quarter of a century to begin to comprehend.

---

[2] Michael Sells, translator, *Approaching the Qur'an: The Early Revelations* (White Cloud Press, 1999), p. 80.

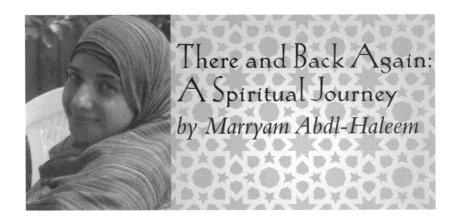

There and Back Again: A Spiritual Journey
by Marryam Abdl-Haleem

Marryam Abdl-Haleem was born in the southwest suburbs of Chicago. She lived there until she was eighteen, when her family decided to move out to rural America (Southwestern Wisconsin). They started a small family farm, where they raised chickens, goats, lambs, turkeys, and ducks. Marryam has eight siblings: five brothers and three sisters. She graduated from University of Wisconsin-Madison with a double major in comparative literature and philosophy. Marryam recently began her PhD at the same school, focusing on Gaelic, French, and Arabic literature. Social justice has played and continues to play a major role in her studies and writing. Through studying these literatures, Marryam hopes to contribute to the voices calling for a more just world. She also recently married the man of her dreams.

I whisked the dark blue book off the shelf, eager to begin. The title promised an intense read: *Remembrance of Death and the Afterlife*. That should have also made me wary of what I was to find inside its covers. It did not. Sixteen-year-old suburban middle-class girls do not, as a rule, take seriously their vague notions of death or the afterlife. Through this book, however, the great Muslim scholar Imam al-Ghazali quickly put an end to that attitude for me.

His words shocked me into realizing my rather shaky reality: I was a mortal being trapped in a mortal world. I was going to die. I freaked out.

Within a week of starting the book, I became thoroughly convinced that I was dying on a daily if not hourly basis. In such moments, I'd break out into a sweat and wait in wide-eyed horror for the Angel of Death to materialize before me and take my soul, thus ending my life forever. Faced with the finality of death, I did what any sophisticated suburbanite would do: I cocooned myself in total denial. With admirable presence of mind, I carried out a rigorous and methodical program of distraction—friends, family, movies, and food. Whatever it bloody well took.

Of course, I could have just stopped reading the book. But I began it for a reason. I had reached that age, the brink of adulthood, when the soul longs for truth and the heart yearns for meaning. So I did not stop.

During this tenuous time, my parents had taken me out of my regular school and enrolled me in an online high school. I decided to use my newfound freedom to travel. I left my safe suburban haven for the bare openness of the ancient city of Cairo.

I fell in love with Cairo. But I also experienced the inevitable feeling of isolation that accompanies foreigners in a new place. I was a stranger in a land I did not call home, surrounded by customs that were not mine and a language I barely knew.

This stark atmosphere sobered me up from the material high of my American life. Back home, I fully depended on my filled-to-the-brim schedule, the helter-skelter of my neverending visits, parties, games, and other entertainment. In Cairo, I had none of that. I only had myself for company.

I no longer had the luxury of someone looming over me, telling me what to do and when. Nor did I have the ease of a readymade routine to plug into along with everybody else. I was forced for the first time to think things out on my own terms, to choose for myself what I should do. I started paying far more attention to each task, asking why it was important and what its purpose was. My heart slowly filled with an ever-increasing anxiety that I needed, right now, to make sense of my actions and my life.

This time, I could not ignore Ghazali's vivid words. They fit perfectly. Life was passing. I physically felt the moments falling away. But where was I headed? I knew my existence could not end with this life. This was only the beginning. For surely I was a being with a heart and a consciousness of right and wrong, with an impetus to strive and succeed. It could not all be for nothing. So what was my purpose?

Such were my thoughts as I wandered through the crowded Cairo streets, my comfortably narrow, superficial subsistence fading away. I was heartbroken. Heartbroken because I felt absolutely alone, surrounded as I was by other powerless beings like myself. Heartbroken because the world I was in love with was fleeting, dreamlike. I also felt fear for I knew I was responsible and accountable. I dreaded the accountability and felt oppressed by the responsibility to make my life worthwhile.

But relief did come. It came from prayer. I never thought to look there for solace, despite the fact that I was raised in a practicing Muslim family and lived my whole life in a religious community. Perhaps this was because I had always performed prayer (and all other acts of worship) just as I did everything else in life: with little or no reflection as to why. I just did them because I was Muslim and that's what religious people did. Besides that, prayer, until this point, had no bearing on my day-to-day life. It had no practical value.

My distress over my mortality and my anxiety about my purpose changed that. I continued to pray. This time I prayed not because that's what Muslims did, but because I desperately needed to talk to God. I felt so lonely and estranged from the world around me that nothing would else suffice. Nothing would console me other than communicating with God directly. For the first time, I linked religious acts with the purpose of fulfilling my overwhelming spiritual needs, of giving transcendent meaning to a transient life.

As I continued to pray with this newfound consciousness, it dawned on me that God chose to create me, specifically, when He did not have to. This realization deeply touched me. He knows me, I remember thinking with relief. I wasn't some insignificant, unknown speck lost in a massive universe. I was personally known and watched over by God. And He gave me a way—prayer—to communicate directly to Him. So even though my material world of comfort collapsed, I gained a more precise perspective on my existence. I was a transcendent being capable of spiritually connecting with my Creator.

A whole new world opened before me. I now noticed how enchanted and filled with life our world truly was. Beauty thrived everywhere I looked. All throughout nature were living, conscious, and spiritual beings. We were connected by our common identity as creatures of God.

The multihued sky enveloped me with calmness. The trees on our streets hovered above me on my walks, my emotional sentinels. I breathed more freely surrounded by the soft rustling of their leaves. My anxiety lifted whenever I studied the delicate shadows shimmering in the spaces of their light. The barren, red rocky landscape encircling Cairo anchored me. Yes, its life, too, was ending, but it was far older than I, and wiser. So I let its beauty and perfection capture me, holding me in its secure embrace.

Still, something was missing. Yes, I felt a strong spiritual connection with God and felt the spiritual energy of His natural world, but I was still living in a physical world with concrete concerns. I distinctly remember feeling the need for (and absence of) palpable, direct communication from the Divine. Our relationship was still too one-sided. I needed Him to speak to me. And I told Him so during and outside my prayers.

It happened again with a book. Sitting in the study—a spacious room with warm-colored throw rugs, deep mahogany furniture, and wall-to-wall bookshelves—I begged God quietly, "If only there was a way for You to talk to me, tell me exactly what I have to do. What exactly do you want from me?"

The answer struck with sudden force. The Book I had been reading from nearly every day in my prayers comprised the verbatim words of God. Weren't they? I felt stunned at how blinded I had been. Those words were divine communication—to me. God was speaking personally to me, to all of us. I couldn't believe it was that obvious.

So I took up the Book and walked out to the balcony. It was sunset in Cairo. The fiery sky flamed purple and pink, yellow and orange: a blazing promise of perfection. I opened the Book and began reading those beautiful, melodious words. They played on my tongue as I spoke them with an intention I never fully had before: to hear and respond to the Divine, material guidance sent for sacred beings—humankind. Quite magically, those enchanted words took root at my core. Like the ritual prayer, reading these words was a far more profound act than simply fulfilling "an Islamic duty." These words would guide me through life's trials and lift me out of its debasing confines. I felt totally free, for I knew with all my heart and soul that I was not alone, trapped by my clay composition. None of us were.

It was a grueling six-month boot camp for a young girl to endure, especially on her own. As my trip neared its end, I felt the satisfying exhaustion one feels during an extensive workout. Just as after any good exercise, I felt such sweet relief when it ended and I found my plane landing at O'Hare Airport. I was home.

But I wasn't really. For, like all others who leave home, I never truly returned. I returned to memories, walking ghostlike through familiar halls. Home no longer held the intense bond it used to. Now, seven years later, I live hundreds of miles away from that place I once called home.

The loss of this bond saddens me sometimes. But the sadness sweetens when I remember my gain. For I learned in my meditative cave called Cairo that home is where the soul is. And my soul is in the Hands of my Lord. We can always be home. And home can be forever.

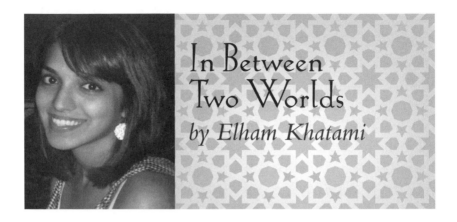

In Between
Two Worlds
by Elham Khatami

Elham Khatami is a reporter for Congressional Quarterly *in Washington, DC. She is a 2009 graduate of the University of Pittsburgh, where she studied political science, writing, and French and served as an editor for the college newspaper,* The Pitt News. *Elham has won collegiate writing awards from the Columbia Scholastic Press Association and the Pennsylvania Newspaper Association. While serving as an intern for CNN and the* Pittsburgh Post-Gazette, *she covered the June 2009 Iranian election fallout. Elham enjoys reading, writing, hiking, and traveling and aspires to become a foreign correspondent.*

"Elham, Elham, *bidar sho*," my father whispers in my ear. "Wake up for morning prayer." He nudges my shoulder gently, and I gaze at his silhouette through my half-open lids.

At nine years old, I have just begun praying five times a day. Facing Mecca, I recite verses in Arabic that, at my young age, are well beyond my comprehension. It is the first thing I do when I come home from school, the first thing I remember when the sun goes down. When I stand beneath my *chador*, the loose fitting robe that covers me head to toe, and assume my serious expression—brows slightly furrowed, eyes down—I feel like a grown-up.

Yet waking before sunrise, groggy and moody, to say hello to God is too much of a hassle for me.

"Why can't we just do our *namaz* (prayers) when we wake up in the morning?" I ask my parents as I stumble out of bed.

"Elham *jaan*,"[1] my father replies, "we must remember Allah at all times, even in the early morning."

My parents came to America by plane, but I was rooted in the Land of the Free. I woke up American in a San Francisco hospital in December 1986. Five months earlier, my parents and one-year-old sister Maryam had left Iran, unsure of when or if they would ever return. They abandoned the busy, bustling streets of Tehran, kissed the tear-stained faces of relatives and friends, and hoped for a life of ease and opportunity in America.

My mother chose to name me "Elham," a word of Arabic origin referring to the inspiring revelation of the Qur'an to the Prophet Muhammad. Every week when my father and I sat down to recite the Qur'an, I would often come across my name hidden among the mélange of Arabic words I did not understand.

"Please, please, please let me change it! Just for school, I swear!" I beg my mother to let me change my name.

Not only do I have difficulty explaining its meaning to my elementary school friends—many of whom have never even heard of the Prophet Muhammad—but I also have trouble teaching them to pronounce it. No, it's not *El-ham* (like the lunch meat), *Ellem*, or *A-lahm*. The closest they can come to pronouncing it correctly is *L-hom*. But they still separate my name into two distinct syllables. It sounds much more beautiful when my mother pronounces it the Iranian way, fusing the 'l' and the 'h' in a unified embrace.

---

[1] A Persian term of endearment meaning one's soul or spirit.

I hate being *L-hom*. I hate the way it sounds. I hate that the kids tease me, that the teachers pause when they reach my name during roll call. Besides my olive skin, bushy eyebrows, and thick, dark hair, my name is the most annoying and obvious reminder of my difference.

"How about Ellen or Elizabeth?" I plead. "Or Elaina or Eleanor?" But my mother simply shakes her head at each suggestion until I eventually give up and storm angrily away to my room.

It is easier to be Elham at home, where I speak Farsi, where I pray to God, where I am not reminded of my differences. And my parents make every effort to maintain this Iranian Muslim environment.

Like most immigrants, my parents live in constant nostalgia of the country they left behind. They cling to tradition as if it is their only salvation in the land of the "Great Satan." The theocratic Shiite Iran has been replaced with a corrupt and impure America. My mother and father realize my sister and I are vulnerable to change, to a loss of Islamic identity they could never bear to witness.

So they preserve traditional Islamic norms, if only for fear of losing their daughters to the West. I am taught to pray and fast during Ramadan. I am encouraged to one day wear hijab. My parents instill in my sister and me the Islamic values of modesty, generosity, and honesty. At school—where I am not allowed to wear shorts, attend school dances, or date and where I wish so much to belong, to hang out at the mall and to go to sleepovers— I try to accept my differences with grace. This is who you are— Muslim, I tell myself.

I soon realize living up to these expectations is not always easy.

"Oh, you're going, you're going," my best friend says, smiling. We're juniors in high school, sitting on the bleachers at the football game, discussing the possibility of going to the school dance. A whistle sounds in the distance, and I pretend to be distracted.

But she keeps pushing. "Come on, it's so much fun!"

I consider lying, telling her that dancing isn't really my thing, that I would rather go home after the game. I contemplate telling her my parents would be disappointed in me. I think of explaining to her that dancing in front of *namahram* boys, boys who are not blood relatives, is wrong in the eyes of God. Instead, I decide I don't really agree with that.

"Ok, let's go," I say, slapping my thighs triumphantly.

After the game, we walk to the high school with the rest of the students. I am surrounded by their excitement, their laughter. I lose myself in the crowd and decide that, just for tonight, I will be one of them. But, in the pit of my stomach, I feel uneasy. If my parents found out, they would disapprove. As we approach the high school, I hear the music; I see the smiling faces of students. My desire to be a part of them is much greater than my fear.

As I try to assimilate myself into American society, my name is sometimes a heavy weight to shoulder. It comes loaded with meaning and thwarts my efforts at finding comfort in my own individual self. I am always reminded of my Muslim identity. Wherever I have gone, whatever I have done, Islam has followed me, persistent and unwilling to let go.

But at the same time, I have been equally unwilling to let *it* go.

Part of the struggle—the jihad, if you will—of growing up Muslim in America is that desperate need to reconcile American culture with Islamic culture, to merge your present with your parents' past. I strive to find my place between home and school, Farsi and English, Iran and America, God and MTV. I want both worlds. I want the freedom promised me by America, and I want the enriching values of Islam.

It takes time, much guilt-ridden time, but I slowly push the restrictions away until I am free. I shrug my parents' Iranian traditions off my shoulders, rid my world of the dogmatic rules that have, for so long, clouded my faith. Sometimes I have trouble looking my parents in the eyes with the knowledge that, after years of following their teachings, the decisions I now make do not always correspond with their beliefs. Sometimes I feel ashamed. I wake up some mornings with the fear—that overwhelming fear—that they are disappointed in me, in the woman I have become. As illogical as it sounds, this fear consumes me. And despite my independence and adulthood, I feel void of strength, unsure who I truly am without my parents' constant validation.

Growing up means shaking loose the ties that bind you so you can finally see your true self—uninfluenced, unburdened you. It means questioning the beliefs that have anchored you all of your life and, however painful it may be, realizing they were never your beliefs to begin with. For most of my life, I found my conscience in my parents—not in God, not in myself. Only now, with this understanding, can I guiltlessly accept my discomfort, trapped in between two worlds, unable to choose … I don't want to have to choose.

Muslim-American. It's not easy, but I learn to unite the words together.

I decide to follow a brand of Islam I can comfortably adapt to my lifestyle in America. With more than one billion Muslims living in the world, all infinitely diverse with different beliefs and ways of life, adaptability is truly the beauty of Islam. It is versatile and ever-changing, not strict and rigid. While I have lost a little religion, I have never lost my faith. I have learned to accept my dual identities, neither of which is complete. And I always remember God.

Now in college, I have my first boyfriend. He has curly blond hair and piercing blue eyes, and his name is so American, it can be found in history books and on museum plaques labeling the statues and portraits of famous historical figures. I sit next to him on the bright orange couch in his apartment, the Qur'an sitting in my lap. We've decided, on a whim, to read it together this summer. Who knows, maybe we're just bored.

"In the Name of Allah, the most Gracious, the most Merciful," I begin reciting aloud. He puts his arm around me as I read, tracing the curve of my shoulder with his fingers. "All the praises and thanks be to Allah, the Lord of the worlds," I continue reading, my voice clear and proud.

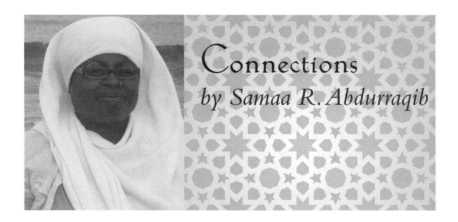

Connections
by Samaa R. Abdurraqib

Samaa R. Abdurraqib graduated from the University of Wisconsin–Madison with a PhD in English, specializing in gender and women's studies. She is currently a visiting assistant professor of gender and women's studies at Bowdoin College. Samaa's research interests include twentieth and twenty-first century American literature, diaspora, and violence against women. She has also written articles on the intersections between African American identity and Muslim identity. Samaa's writing has been published in the books Muslim Voices in School: Narratives of Identity and Pluralism; Arab Voices in Diaspora: Critical Perspectives on Anglophone Arab Literature; *and* Teaching Against Islamophobia.

It was difficult for me to be a Muslim when I was growing up. This wasn't because the US's so-called secular society made it complicated. It was because I couldn't figure out how to fit in and still be Muslim. I didn't grow up with Muslim friends. There were few Muslims in the midwestern city my family settled in after moving from New York City. Most of the Muslims we knew in this new city were Arab immigrants or Arab American.

My mother and I failed to find a niche for ourselves in these circles. We didn't fit in. We didn't speak Arabic, and we were African-American. When I was among other Muslims, I felt I was constantly being judged: my skin color, my mannerisms, my clothing, the way I wore hijab—they were all wrong. I felt as if I was not the right kind of Muslim.

When I was younger, I thought these reactions occurred because they could sense my slight ambivalence about religion. Being Muslim meant I had to practice and present myself in a certain way, especially if I wanted to have a place in a Muslim community. It wasn't until much later in life that I was able to relate my earlier difficulties connecting to Islam to my lack of connection with a Muslim community.

Back then, I felt practicing Islam was, in many ways, a hardship. I was angry because I wasn't allowed to attend parties and concerts like the rest of my friends. And I remember thinking how unfair and cruel it was that I wasn't allowed to have boyfriends. I resented wearing hijab, praying felt like a tedious drain on my social life, and fasting breath was an embarrassment.

So I rebelled in small ways: I cut classes, I skipped school, I lied, and I moped. I went through periods where I would stop praying altogether and lie about it when asked. I would "cheat" during Ramadan and snatch bites of food. If caught, I claimed I'd forgotten I was supposed to be fasting. I stopped being concerned about whether other Muslims thought I was "Muslim enough" and became more concerned about what my non-Muslim peers thought about me.

But my peers couldn't understand my differences, either. They made fun of me, my hijab, my name.... Yet I continued to try to fit in: I made up stories about parties and music concerts I'd attended and complicated relationships with boys who didn't go to my school. Because Islam was a source of discomfort for me rather than a source of pride and strength, it was easy for me to lie instead of explaining the religious reasons why I was different from my friends and classmates.

Internally, however, I didn't exactly feel any compulsion to be spiritually connected to Islam. I did feel a sense of obligation to at least give the appearance of being a practicing Muslim. This sense of obligation mostly stemmed from respect for my parents and how hard they'd worked to raise me as a Muslim. As a young teenager, I knew of young Muslim women who wore their hijabs as they left their houses for school but took them off as soon as they were out of their parents' sight. I was sure their frustrations with wearing hijab weren't that different from mine. Yet I was horrified by their boldness. I knew if my parents had caught me audaciously defying their rules, it would make them feel as if I had no respect for them.

At the time, Islam had no real meaning for me. I didn't understand spirituality, so Islam was mostly a set of rules enforced by my parents. My commitment to practicing Islam was really just a commitment to my parents. I knew they wanted me to pray, so I would pray when they were around. I knew if I stopped wearing hijab once I left the house, they would find out immediately, so I never removed my hijab in public.

I didn't experience a moment of epiphany that helped me understand spirituality. I never went searching for it. My spirituality evolved when I was looking for something else. When I started college, I decided to find a religious community of my own. Islam, in general, felt familiar to me because I'd been Muslim all of my life, yet on another level, I felt a certain discomfort with Islam. Practicing Islam marginalized me in non-Muslim communities, yet I didn't exactly fit into the Muslim communities my family had found in the past. Lack of community made it difficult for me to practice because, other than my immediate family, I didn't have any personal connections to any Muslims. If I had, I would have felt less guilt over my conflicted feelings about practicing. Eventually finding a Muslim community helped me better understand the diversity of religiosity amongst Muslims, which enabled me to move beyond my feelings of guilt and desire to fit in. I also discovered a more fulfilling sense of spirituality. This self-analysis would come later. At that moment, I was just trying to find a place where I could fit in.

I found a different type of Muslim community at my undergraduate university. This community was diverse in terms of ethnicity, race, and country of origin, as well as degree of religiosity. I began my search for a community with the MSA (Muslim Student Association). I can't recall exactly how or why I ended up at an MSA meeting, but I remember worrying I would face the same ostracization I'd experienced among other Muslims when I was younger. I didn't quite find the community I had envisioned—however, I did find a smaller group of Muslims who helped me feel comfortable with my Islam.

Rather than dwelling on intense and anxiety-producing questions (to wear or not to wear hijab, to pray two *rakats sunnah* or not to pray sunnah, and so on), my new friends and I spent time reading the Qur'an. We talked about how being Muslim and practicing Islam fit in with our current lives. Several of my friends had, like me, been through ups and downs with their Islam. They'd experienced days, weeks, or months when they weren't spiritually inspired, had not prayed, failed to fast, or went through the motions of Islamic ritual without enthusiasm. I also met friends who had practiced unwaveringly their entire lives. These friends helped me understand that, sometimes, Muslims vacillate between levels of religiosity, and that doesn't mean they're any more or less Muslim.

Being around this group taught me how to be proud of and unapologetic for being Muslim, regardless of who was around. These friends' acceptance of me as I was showed me that, while being a part of a larger community is important, it was more important to find people who don't expect me to be a certain type of Muslim. They helped me move past my concerns about outward expressions of my religiosity. I stopped thinking about how the way I practiced appeared to others and focused more on how Islam connected me to God.

This community helped me feel better about who I was as a Muslim. They helped me stop negating the parts of myself that hadn't seemed quite right in the past. I spent more time focusing on the positive aspects of Islam and being Muslim. We talked about spirituality rather than behavior; we talked about the beauty of being a Muslim woman rather than the restrictions; we talked about the benefits of being in America and practicing Islam rather than the hardships. Islam became more than just simple and meaningless obedience to me. I learned Islam was about nurturing a strong connection with God, and that strong connection is what spawned my obedience. I began to understand Islam was not about practicing one way—religion was broad enough to encompass different forms of religious expression. Although some other Muslims might not accept me because I did not "fit" their idea of what a proper Muslim should look and act like, it grew clear to me that God accepted me as the Muslim I actually was.

I began to realize how much more there was to Islam and being Muslim than just the rules I'd felt had dictated my life earlier. It was no longer as important to me if other Muslims felt I wasn't, for example, wearing my hijab "properly." I knew my circle of friends was more concerned about me as a person and how I expressed my love for Islam than what I looked like or said. I can, with a degree of certainty, say I would've been spiritually and religiously lost if I hadn't found this group of Muslim friends.

That isn't to say that during that time, or even now, my life doesn't contain contradictions or inconsistencies. This doesn't mean I read the Qur'an every day, always pray on time, visit the mosque regularly, or enthusiastically fast each Ramadan. During college, however, I transitioned to a stage of my life where Islam became important—more important than being able to fit in among Muslims or non-Muslims.

Islam, for me, began to center on my spirituality and connection with God. It is this connection with God that compels my actions—Islamic practices and otherwise. It is my ongoing relationship with the group of Muslims I met in college that continues to affirm, sustain, and validate the person I am as a Muslim. And in turn, these connections with God and my friends have allowed me to be more comfortable with myself and my practice as a Muslim.

Hyphenated Identity
by Naheed Hamid

Naheed Hamid earned her bachelor's degree in microbiology, immunology, and molecular genetics from UCLA. She is currently completing her master's of public health in epidemiology at UCLA while finishing up her first year of medical school at Western University of Health Sciences. A champion of humanitarian causes, Naheed is an activist in the Afghan American community. On her free time, she enjoys painting, traveling, hiking, and attempting to learn how to play the rubab, the national instrument of Afghanistan.

Sitting in my history class on the first day of school, I wait patiently while the teacher calls our names. Since our class seemed so diverse, my teacher had suggested the students state their ethnic backgrounds as an icebreaker. One by one, he calls out the names, and one by one, the students share their ethnicities.

"Mateo Alvarez?"

"Present. I'm Mexican American."

"Hillary Johnson?"

"Present. My family is of English and Irish descent."

"Payman Mohajeri?"

"Present. I'm Iranian American."

On and on my teacher continues as I nervously prepare my response.

"Maryam Yazid—"

"Present. I'm also Iranian American."

"Kimberly Marfori?"

"Present. My parents are from the Philippines."

I'm next.

"Naheed Hamid?"

"Present. I'm Afghan."

"Oh, African? Which part?"

"No. I'm Afghan. As in from Afghanistan."

"I see. Wow, I've never met an Afghan before!"

The usual series of questions follows, ranging from how long I've lived in America to what the situation is like in Afghanistan. I don't mind these questions. I enjoy explaining the situation in Afghanistan and what it was like before all the chaos. This kind of questioning doesn't involve any preconceived notions about the Afghan people. It shows me people are interested and want to learn and aren't basing their knowledge of Afghanistan solely on what they may have heard from word of mouth or television. It makes me feel good when I can clear up any confusion or destroy any stereotypes that exist about Afghans, Muslims, and Afghan Muslim Women.

I didn't always feel comfortable or knowledgeable enough to talk about Afghanistan or Islam to curious strangers. When I was growing up, my parents taught me the basic tenets of Islam. Once in a while, I would hear stories about Afghanistan but not enough to appease the inquiring minds of fellow classmates or friends. September 11, 2001 was a defining moment for me, as it was for many Muslims. I was in high school at about the age when people start trying to understand who they are and which of their values set them apart from their parents.

After September 11, the world's view of Islam and Afghanistan was redefined in a way that differed from the picture my parents had painted for me. Islam became associated with terrorism, and Afghanistan was seen as a backwards, barbaric nation that needed to be bombed back to the Stone Age. The images I saw on television weren't the images I associated with my religion or the land of my ancestors. The Islam I was taught by my father was a tolerant and peaceful religion, a religion without compulsion. The Afghanistan my parents spoke about was an advancing nation with beautiful gardens and mulberry trees and whose people had values, aspirations, hospitality, understanding, and compassion.

Seeing images of innocent Afghan civilians caught in yet another power struggle was heartbreaking. Their situation seemed very real to me. It's easy to feel disconnected when all you do is hear or read about the situation. Yet I saw the images of my family in the faces of those civilians, and I felt pulled toward them. Because of the disparity between the media's depiction of Afghanistan and the Afghanistan my parents had reminisced about, I felt compelled to do some research on my own. Not only did I educate myself on the situation in Afghanistan and its history following the Soviet invasion, but I also became more knowledgeable about Islam.

Although I had followed many of the tenets of Islam since my childhood, it was a blind following. I dressed modestly, fasted during Ramadan, and prayed properly because that's what I had always known. It was just the way things were supposed to be done. It wasn't until I did my own research on Islam that I became more spiritual. That's when I began to appreciate the religion and understand the reasoning behind the tenets. I awakened to the country of my roots as well as to my religion.

As one of the few Afghan Muslims in my school, I became the face of Afghan Muslim women for my classmates, teachers, and even strangers. I wanted to make sure I could answer their questions and clear up any misconceptions they had about my culture or my religion. I had to explain why my father didn't make me wear a scarf and how my family felt about women getting an education. I also clarified that Islam does not promote terrorism or the mistreatment of women. The more I had to explain my culture and my religion, the less "American" I felt, despite having been born in America. I began to feel closer ties to a country I had never even visited than to the country of my birth. In America, I didn't feel like I belonged. I was viewed as an outsider, so I accepted that role.

Meanwhile, learning about the deteriorating situation in Afghanistan was frustrating. I wanted to do something to help, but I just didn't know how to get involved. The only thing I could do was start off small. Getting involved in nonprofit organizations gave me a little satisfaction and made me feel somewhat useful.

When I started attending UCLA in fall 2003, I became involved in the Afghan Students Association. We did what we could to raise awareness about the situation in Afghanistan. We put on culture shows, sold clothing, and conducted school supply drives to raise funds for the Midwife Clinic Project of the Afghanistan Relief Organization.

There are many issues facing the Afghan people, but the one that has struck the deepest chord for me is health care. Even before September 11, I was aware of the mistreatment of women under the Taliban. It sickened me to hear about the lack of health care for women and people in general. The rate of Afghan women who die while giving birth is one of the highest in the world. Social justice is something I have always been passionate about, and the inequality between men and women in Afghanistan under the Taliban angered me.

I didn't understand the reasoning behind the ban on education for girls in Afghanistan and the lack of proper health care.

None of this had anything to do with Islam or Afghan culture. It was unacceptable. Growing up, I was always taught people are equal regardless of race, gender, or class, and it upset me to think that years of war had made the nation go backwards when it came to basic rights. As passionate as I was about extinguishing these disparities between men and women in Afghanistan, I knew politics was not an arena I wanted to enter. Instead, I felt the best way for me to help the Afghan people was to become involved in health care, inspiring my passion for medicine.

After learning so much about the situation in Afghanistan, I felt it was my duty to do something about it—not because of a nationalistic pride, but because I could have just as easily been in that situation if my parents hadn't been lucky enough to be able to leave. Because I had the privilege of growing up in an environment where I didn't have to dodge bombs, I have an obligation to help those who don't have access to those opportunities.

A few years ago, I was at a point where I was identifying only with my Afghan roots. I told people I was from Afghanistan, even though I had never visited there. I considered myself more Afghan than American, despite being born in the US. This was mainly because of the disconnect I felt between myself and the society I was living in. Society perceived my religion as a threat and my Afghan culture as irrational.

My drive to improve the situation in Afghanistan comes not only from the concern I have for the welfare of its people but also from the basic American ideals I have been taught by living in this country. Being exposed to the notion of equality for all people—regardless of race, gender, religion, or class—made me champion humanitarian causes and the rights of Afghan women. Realizing my passion to help the Afghan people is due largely to the values cherished by the American people has helped me accept my hyphenated identity. I can now truly and proudly say I am an Afghan American.

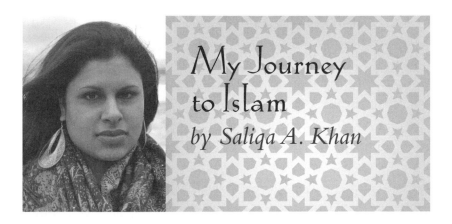

My Journey to Islam
by Saliqa A. Khan

Saliqa A. Khan is a digital journalist for a leading Internet news company. During her professional tenure, Saliqa has broken and covered some of the nation's most gripping news stories. She continues to seek innovative ways to tell a compelling story with multimedia panache. Saliqa works closely with Grammy Award–nominated artists and music industry producers on independent projects. Often expressing herself through poetry and spoken word, she is a rebel at heart who enjoys walking the thin line and occasionally crossing it to bring awareness to injustices. Saliqa firmly believes the pen is mightier than the sword. She strives to always give back in some form, starting with her family and extending to those in need. Saliqa feels blessed with the wisdom to see the silver lining in almost any negative situation. She truly believes God knows best. For more information on Saliqa and her work, visit her website at www.saliqa.com.

My journey to Islam began with the end of my marriage. During my marriage, I would look at myself in the mirror and hear my mother's voice saying, "Remember who you are. Never forget who you are." Then I would ask myself, "Who am I?"

I thought I knew. I was an energetic person, a social butterfly who was ambitious about her dreams and motivated to bring them to fruition. That determination had been a part of me since I was very young, but I'd lost that strength over the course of my abusive marriage. Rediscovering this aspect of myself—finding *me* again—was one of the most difficult challenges of my life

I am a first-generation American Muslim woman of Pakistani Afghani descent who was married to a reverted Puerto Rican Muslim. Initially, our marriage ruffled a lot of feathers in both of our families. Yet our marriage lasted for nearly a decade, through good times and bad. Towards the end, however, the bad times outnumbered the good.

During our marriage, I was becoming closer to my Islam. I was tired of struggling, being a young mom, going to college, and working two jobs as the breadwinner of the family. It was taking a toll on me. I didn't believe in using medication to alleviate my stress, and I stubbornly thought I didn't need anyone to lean on.

Boy, was I wrong. I did need someone, but the obvious choice—my husband—wasn't there for me. I voiced concerns to him, and he brushed me off like I was invisible. I held my marriage vows sacred, so I didn't even consider seeking a confidante outside of that bond. Even my family didn't quite understand my world of hurt. I finally gave up—and gave in to God.

It was Ramadan, and we were going through tough times. There was nothing to eat in our home. I went to school thinking, "What am I going to feed my kids tonight?" *Alhumdulillah*, I was heard. God listened to me. After an Iftar dinner on campus, members of the Muslim Student Association (MSA) insisted I take home the leftovers, even though no one knew my situation at home. I hesitated at first but pushed my pride aside and thought, "*This* is for my kids." We had food for a week. As heavy as it was, my heart smiled.

Slowly but surely, things became a little better. I worked more hours, started a second job, and received a better financial aid package with funds for living expenses. This alleviated some of the financial burden that had been weighing on my shoulders. At the same time, I was becoming stronger in my Islam. While these aspects of my life improved, my relationship with my husband deteriorated.

With my strengthening faith, the financial stress and other burdens felt lighter and more manageable. I prayed more frequently and on time, read more of the Qur'an, attended MSA-sponsored events, and sought the company of fellow Muslim students for support and comfort. I genuinely put my trust in God as Islam told me to, and that allowed me to let go of my immediate insecurities and day-to-day stress. As I drew closer to God, my husband became more deviant. We literally were at odds with each other. My husband didn't voice his dislike for my deepening relationship with Islam, but his actions indicated how he really felt.

It took me a while to realize our marriage was over. It had been for a while. I planned my exit by literally mapping out how and when I would leave, beginning with a phone call to mom. She had witnessed the friction in our marriage when she visited in person, so I knew she would understand.

Leaving was easier said than done. First I needed confirmation, so I prayed on it. I wanted God to grant me permission to get a divorce. I needed a sign. I needed something. The long walks from the shuttle bus to our apartment gave me time to contemplate the possible signs, but nothing jumped out. I studied the trees swaying in the wind and wondered what the sign would be.

My husband was a fully able man who, instead of working, had chosen to pursue a music career that ultimately failed. I wanted to support his dream, but there was no effort on his part to provide for his family. He felt my decision to go to school meant I should bear the weight. I could no longer justify his actions or the physical, mental, and emotional abuse. The more I learned about life and especially my *deen*, the more jealous he became. I finally saw the man I married for who he really was. Seriously, had I been *that* stupid?

I knew I needed to go, but I kept finding reasons to stay—namely, the kids. I didn't want them to lose their father, and I didn't want to be a bad mother. I wanted to keep this family together, the family I had worked so hard to raise. In the end, it was my kids who opened my eyes. Finally, God had given me my sign.

I was leaving for school one morning dressed in hijab and full Islamic gear. The kids were cheerfully eating breakfast at the kitchen table. Their happy mood made me happy, too. I headed to the door to make my exit. I hugged and kissed my kids goodbye, skipping my husband because I knew he was in a bad mood. I had wanted to avoid a confrontation. "Have a good day, everyone!" I said as I reached the door.

"You're not going to give me a goodbye kiss?" he yelled.

I replied, "Look, I don't want to fight. I'm running late. I'm sorry."

"You're not going anywhere," he said, grabbing my hijab and pulling me to the ground. This time, his disrespect had extended to God. I had the sign I needed. My son ran up and asked, "Dad, why did you pull mommy's hijab off her head?" My husband said, "I didn't pull it. She fell." My son said, "Daddy, you're lying. I just saw you."

My heart was crushed and at the same time, proud. One of my gifts from God, my six-year-old son, had stood up for Mommy. My little man did what any good Muslim man would do: protect the women in your family. How ironic, I thought, for my Muslim son to defend me against his so-called Muslim father. Months later, my children and I mustered the courage to leave. I realized the only one I should ever really fear is God.

My marriage was failing, but my Islam wasn't. Out of one of the weakest moments in life had emerged something even stronger. How many signs did God need to give me? The fact that I awakened every day was sign enough that God was giving me another chance to make things right.

Even after I left, I wondered at the back of my mind whether I should do this to my children. I still needed confirmation that I made the right decision, so my brother and I went to see a sheikh. I needed a learned Muslim to advise me, but I have to admit I was embarrassed to describe the situation I was in and what I had gone through. As naive as it sounds, I thought I was the only one. I can clearly remember feeling at peace in the mosque. I was nervous the sheikh would judge me, but God never ceases to amaze me. The sheikh listened to me with extreme attentiveness. He gave me what Islam permitted: grounds for divorce. He even offered to speak to my estranged husband to solidify the decision. After our meeting, the sheikh confirmed my own thoughts by saying, "You had eight reasons for a valid divorce. Why didn't you leave sooner?" Suddenly, I felt an enormous burden of guilt lifted from my shoulders.

Three months after leaving with the kids, I got a phone call from my estranged husband. He told me he was expecting a child with another woman. When I got off the phone, I was hurt. I cried a lot. If there was even a morsel of hope that we could reconcile, this phone call destroyed it.

It has been five years since we left, and my children's father has only called a handful of times. He has not sent one cent of child support or even seen his children.

Hindsight is always 20/20. All I had to do was let go and find me again. I had to put my trust in God. Since then, I've become a much better mother. Despite tough times, I am more financially stable. I know my kids are growing up Muslim; they are not lost. When my kids see me, they see inspiration. And they, in turn, inspire me. They teach me about Islam when they read *surahs*, correct my mannerisms, or tell me about hadiths I have yet to learn. My three beautiful seeds and I are all blossoming together.

They say divorce is like a death. Islam gave me back my life.

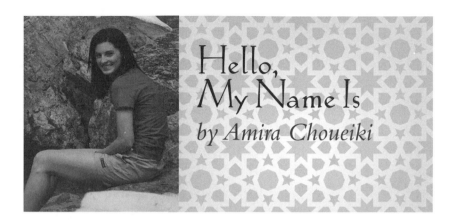

Hello,
My Name Is
by Amira Choueiki

Amira Choueiki was born in Columbus, Ohio, and spent some of her childhood in Kuwait City, Kuwait. She currently attends the Georgia Institute of Technology, where she is majoring in economics and international affairs. Amira conducted domestic policy research during an internship in Washington, DC. She also interned at a security and defense think tank in Dubai, United Arab Emirates, where she researched terrorist group recruitment and training. Amira has spent time working with autistic students. She organized a weekly Bible / Qur'an / Torah comparative study with friends of different faiths. With hopes of pursuing a career in education development in the Middle East, Amira strives to serve as an ambassador of both her faith and country. You can follow her adventures or contact her at achoueiki.tumblr.com.

One of our scholarship program advisors at Georgia Tech frequently reminds us that a person's name is the most significant piece of information to know about them. When you call someone by name, that person subconsciously places you in their "friends and family" category. A name is the first thing you learn about a person, and it is how you will always remember them. Your parents placed your name upon you. They associated it with something they saw or hoped for in you, and you grow into it. In a way, a person's name literally defines them.

But what if your name confuses you? What if it's a juxtaposition of two contrasting realms, making you not fully fit into either? Every time I tell someone my name, I go through the same routine, explaining each bit while watching their perplexed facial expressions. I'm prepared for all the usual questions: "Okay, where is that from?", "So what religion are you, exactly?", and "How did that happen?" Sometimes, the questions don't even surface but just linger between a ruffled brow and a tilted head. I usually acknowledge their confusion with a quick, "Oh, my dad's Lebanese," and they generally nod back and say, "Oh, cool."

The struggle with my name began in 1996, when I was in second grade. My parents had decided to move our family to Kuwait, where my father taught at a university during a two-year sabbatical. They wanted my brothers and me—who had only lived in Ohio until that point—to experience an Arab country, sharpen our Arabic language skills, live among people of our faith, and immerse ourselves in our cultural heritage.

Attending the American School of Kuwait (ASK), my brothers and I were surprised to find students and teachers representing seventy-four different nationalities at the school. Although everyone got along well at ASK, there was definitely a fine line between the American and Arab students attending the school. Two groups formed: The American Circle and the Arab Circle. There was a "we're-the-Americans" consciousness that most children of military and oil company employees possessed. This was not difficult to observe, even for an eight-year-old.

I also knew we had not moved across the world so I could hang out with peers exactly like those at home in America. I was here to become acquainted with Arab students and the Arab way of life. I made fast friends with the local population and loved spending time with them. Frequently pulled towards the "cool" American group, I felt torn between two circles of friends.

My family as a whole also felt a dual pull. We did not look forward to going to the military Base Exchange (BX) for pork and beer, but we did visit the embassy for Fourth of July celebrations. My family did not dress in traditional Kuwaiti clothing, but we did appreciate hearing the call for prayer from our neighborhood mosque. I was equally a part of and excluded from the two worlds, and I longed to be accepted in both.

At ASK, Muslim students took a required religion class, while non-Muslims enrolled in an art class. I often thought how much more fun my American friends Lauren and Amanda must be having making pottery than I was memorizing *surahs*. One day, I stepped out of class to get a drink of water. Heading back to my classroom, I bumped into Spencer—the cutest, blondest, blue-eyed American boy in Kuwait City. As we crossed paths, he looked at me and asked, "Amira, where are you going?" From his facial expression, I immediately realized he was confused to see me going to the religion class. He turned around and walked backwards, quickly uttering three words so shocking to me, yet spoken with such innocent naiveté: "But you're American!"

That phrase stung me in a way Spencer never intended. At first, I was almost proud he had recognized me as "one of his kind." It took about three seconds for me to realize the significance of what he had said. He had implied that I had to choose—American *or* Muslim—as if it was impossible to be both. While I knew deep down this wasn't true, his words still hurt and made me feel like even more of an outsider. In one sentence, he called into question everything I had been feeling during our stay in Kuwait, leaving me wondering whom I really was.

As I grew up, I knew no one else like me. Even the Muslims I'd known in Ohio were deeply rooted in their own cultural traditions, usually Pakistani. They had formed a whole community together, one I clearly did not fit into. I could find no peers who were a half-and-half mix like me. I had no examples to follow, no kindreds to discuss my situation with. My Arab cousins didn't understand why I used tampons, and my teammates didn't understand why I fasted during Ramadan when I had volleyball practice or a game. Feeling judged and misunderstood by both ends of the spectrum, I had no idea how to bridge the two sides.

My family also differed from other Muslim families we knew because of our mixed heritage. My father is Lebanese; my mother is an American of Irish German descent who was raised Catholic. Other kids seemed to see me as "less Muslim" because of my mother. While my father is extremely disciplined in his faith as a Muslim, praying five times a day and attending the mosque frequently, I struggled for a long time with my mother and her faith. She had chosen to raise us Muslim, fasting with us and reminding us when it was prayer time. Yet she still attended Christmas masses with her family. I took this as a personal attack. It felt like she was "cheating" on us. I also resented her for never saying she had "converted," and I hated how she would never say she attested to a specific religion. As I grew older, met more people, and started learning about other faiths, I realized what my mother had been silently preaching to my brothers and me throughout our childhood: her belief in finding commonalities and focusing on the good in people. I now respect my mother more than anyone in the world and recognize her religious teachings have positively impacted me just as much if not more than my father's traditional religious education.

I'd like to say there was a single event that brought me peace, something that ended my internal chaos, but unfortunately no such thing has occurred. Nor do I think it will. This is a gradual, learn-as-you-go process. I now realize there is no right answer. Sometimes you just have to figure it out for yourself.

What is the ideal American Muslim woman? I don't know.

Does she cover her hair? Does she date like her friends do? Can she wear what she wants? There's nothing in the Qur'an that says: "Here's what to do when the American boy you like thinks you can't be American *and* Muslim," or "Here's how to grow up in the United States." There are a lot of other questions the Qur'an hasn't answered for me, like, "Can I just pick the pepperoni off the pizza?", "If I'm at a fraternity mixer and there's alcohol, do I have to leave?" or "Is my volleyball uniform inappropriate because it's spandex?"

I have found the greatest solace in prayer—and increasingly trusting God with each passing year. I can't define all of the answers, but I can hope my relationship with and dependency on Him are sufficient.

One of the most profound blessings in my life has been finding other women like me. At college, I finally met people facing similar hurdles. I derive a sense of peace from this small community to which I belong. There are others who are as confused as I am—and that's okay. We are all working on figuring this out together. We are trying to find the balance between practicing our religion the best way we know how and enjoying life in this wonderful country we were fortunate enough to be born in.

When people ask me now about my name, I say, "It's Amira Elizabeth Choueiki. Choueiki is pronounced *shway-key*. Yeah, it's Lebanese, but it's spelled phonetically in French. And my middle name is Elizabeth because that is what my mom wanted to name her daughter before she married an Arab man. I am a Muslim, but half of my family is Catholic. My three best friends are Methodist, Jewish, and Hindu, and I've found myself trying to fit into the American Midwest, the Middle East, and the American South as I have grown up. Yes, it is complicated and crazy, but just like my name, my life is a mixture of worlds and cultures, and I love it that way."

Ready to Wear
by Nyla Hashmi

Nyla Hashmi was born and raised in Connecticut by an American mother and Pakistani father. Growing up in a progressive yet conservative Muslim household, she was always on the lookout for clothing that both fit the modest dress code while making her feel confident. Nyla decided to begin designing and sewing her own clothing. She earned a bachelor's degree in fashion design from one of the top fashion schools in America, the Fashion Institute of Technology. Nyla has worked alongside top designers in the industry, including Elie Tahari, Oscar de la Renta, Giorgio Armani, and Sean John. She started Eva Khurshid, a women's fashion brand, with longtime friend Fatima Monkush. After three years of building their brand, Nyla and Fatima now sell their line in boutiques across the US and UK.

My life revolves around a hemline. It has defined my career path and given me a point of view. Through fashion, I have refined my outlook on Islam and found a way to balance my multifaceted background. Fashion is my dream, but I had to find the courage to pursue it. It took me years to overcome my sense of feeling torn between my culture, upbringing, and religion.

Growing up, I tried to achieve a balance between my American and Pakistani identities. Between the ages of ten and sixteen, I lived in both Lahore, Pakistan, and Connecticut, US. Much of my youth was spent shuttling back and forth between these two culturally divergent places and two strikingly different identities. At the age of thirteen, I landed back in Connecticut after being in Lahore for three years. I found myself having to adjust to American teenage culture while still conforming to the dress code and lifestyle of a conservative Muslim girl.

The culture shock set in when my mother took me shopping for school. We found only skin-baring tank tops, short shorts, and body-hugging clothing of every form. We were frustrated that we couldn't find anything that covered me up while still remaining somewhat fashionable.

My best friend, our mothers, and I had previously discussed the idea of sewing our own clothing. Both of our mothers grew up sewing their own clothing and were eager to teach Fatima and me. After this shopping trip, we revisited that conversation. At that moment, I experienced an epiphany. I decided that someday I was going to change the world of fashion by creating a modest yet fashionable line of clothing.

Spending the first two years of high school abroad and my last two in Connecticut, I constantly struggled to feel socially accepted among my peers both in America and Pakistan. Often, I ended up confused and alone. In my teenage mind, what I wore, how I acted, and what I did determined whether I was "cool" or not. I stood out among my peers in both countries because of my mixed ethnicity, my conservative Muslim values, and my American upbringing. In America, I started to withdraw from my friends, feeling I had little in common with them anymore. I became closer to other Muslim girls from the community when we realized we were all confronting the same identity issues: we were Muslim girls living in America.

Comforted by my new community of friends, I focused on my goal to design clothes my friends and I could wear. Throughout high school, I studied all of the Italian and French designers and became familiar with the latest trends. Although I was inspired and excited by the newest looks, I still found them beyond the boundaries of Muslim wardrobe. So I created my own stylish yet modest designs, sewed my creations, and wore them to school. People noticed the new and different looks I modeled every day. Designing clothing for myself consisted of a lot of experimenting with fabrics, shapes, construction, and details. One of the first tops I made was a knit tunic with an asymmetric hem extending from my high hip to right above my knee. I even designed and constructed prom dresses for myself and other girls.

During my senior year, I was accepted to the Fashion Institute of Technology. Moving to New York City was inspiring and instrumental to my career. Internships such as the one I held at Oscar de la Renta refined my taste and gave me the keen eye needed to become a successful designer. In fall 2009, Fatima and I finally launched our long-anticipated fashion brand, Eva Khurshid, which encompasses both our fashion philosophy and our Muslim values.

The community of American Muslim friends I found in high school helped me accept my Muslim self. Knowing there were other girls out there like me was comforting. Seeing them struggle with the same issues of balance I faced made me even more determined to pursue the field of fashion. I knew this would be my way of making a difference in their lives. These feelings of empowerment, drive, and passion focused me on my ultimate career goals and, more importantly, gave me peace of mind.

Since launching Eva Khurshid, Fatima and I have received letters from women all over the world sharing their admiration for what we are doing and describing their shared struggles as Muslim women living in Western society. These women's stories motivate me to create even more cutting-edge, modest designs.

Sketching an idea on paper and forging that concept into something tangible is one of the most rewarding experiences of my life. Clothing is a form of self-expression. It's a way to showcase your personality. Being comfortable with how I look and feel boosts my self-confidence.

As a teenager, I learned feeling good about what I wore ultimately helped me feel confident about who I was inside and out. Fashion designing didn't just solve my problem of what to wear—it helped me achieve balance in other areas of my life as well, giving me a sense of peaceful fulfillment. I am, so to speak, more comfortable in my shoes—and my clothes—as a confident, independent, and self-assured woman.

It should come as no surprise that the clothing I design ultimately reflects myself. It is a statement of my style and perceptions of modesty while showing how I choose to blend into American culture as a Muslim. This clothing is created for all types of women, from conservative to liberal Muslims to non-Muslims to anyone who wants to dress modestly yet still express her individuality and style.

Destined to become a designer, I believe in what I am doing. I am passionate about my career and know I have something new and refreshing to offer girls who are facing the same struggles I used to face. My personal philosophy that women should be empowered to do anything has now evolved into my fashion philosophy: women should feel empowered by what they wear. Eva Khurshid redefines what it means to be an empowered, confident woman.

My outlook on Islam combines the conservative principles my parents raised me with and the worldly experiences that have given me an open mind—influences I have been surrounded by throughout my life. For me, it is not as important to go directly by the "book." I am free to create my own interpretation of my religion as well as my fashion. Going into business for myself has taught me to how to make my own rules and still feel comfortable within the value system I was taught. I hope to inspire other young American Muslim women to chase after their dreams as I did.

Today, I am comfortable saying I am American, Pakistani, and Muslim. I am neither the perfect person nor the perfect Muslim, but I know I have achieved a good balance in all that I am. Every hemline of my clothing reflects this, ultimately expressing a seamless coexistence between all of my cherished identities.

Learning Tolerance
by Sevim Sabriye Kalyoncu

The only child of a Turkish father and an American mother, Sevim Sabriye Kalyoncu grew up in Tuscaloosa, Alabama, and the suburbs of Washington, DC. She received her bachelor of science from Georgetown University's Edmund A. Walsh School of Foreign Service, followed by a master of arts in Middle Eastern studies from the University of Chicago. Sevim has worked for various nonprofit organizations in Washington, DC. The University of Chicago Human Rights Program awarded her a grant that allowed her to work in Turkey, where she aided women's organizations in their fight against the country's ban on the Islamic headscarf. She currently lives in Arlington, Virginia, with her husband, Andy Nunez, and works as a freelance editor, specializing in writings that address Islam and the Middle East.

I like to brag about having grown up Muslim in the Bible Belt of the United States of America. It was only thanks to God that I was able to maintain my faith while surrounded by a Southern Baptist majority and a common view of Islam as a warped, if not evil, religion. What made being Muslim in 1980s Tuscaloosa,

Alabama, difficult was having no official Muslim community. That is why I focused on the literal and inclusive definition of a Muslim as "one who submits to God," which allowed me to accept my non-Muslim community as "Muslim." Whether they knew it or not, I viewed my friends as people who "submitted to God" and shared the same faith as me.

When the first Gulf War struck in 1991 and people began to speak badly about Muslims, I felt the need to share what I had understood to be the peaceful, open, and accepting nature of my faith. My eleventh-grade English class was given an assignment to speak on any topic, so I decided to present on "Western Misconceptions about Islam."

On the day of my presentation, I felt excited but nervous. I was shaking as I read aloud what I had written about the meaning of Islam, explaining how Muslims actually believe Jesus had been sent by God to lead humanity. I emphasized that Muslims believe in the same God that Christians and Jews believe in. Speaking for all of the Muslims I knew, I explained our belief that all good Christians, Jews, Muslims, and anyone else who believed in God (whether they used that name or not) would go to heaven—the same heaven.

By the time I finished my speech and the class started asking questions, I felt comfortable standing in front of everyone. Words rolled off my tongue as I described how I prayed and how I had chosen my own faith. With the exception of the students from the Open Door Baptist Church—who had put their heads down on their desks and covered their ears throughout my presentation—people were genuinely interested in what I had to say. I spoke through the entire period, and when the bell rang, the teacher said I could continue answering questions the next day.

As I headed out from school that afternoon, I felt proud to be a Muslim and proud of myself for speaking out about my faith. I knew I had done the right thing by standing up in front of my class, and I felt my efforts—not only to explain the religion of Islam but also to allay people's fears about Muslims—had been well-received.

Amber, a Pakistani American friend who had never spoken openly about being Pakistani or Muslim, ran up to tell me that rumors were being spread about me. In reaction to my talk, one of the classmates who had refused to listen had accused me of being in Saddam Hussein's army. Amber joked about how we were supposedly hiding machine guns in our tiny purses, but neither she nor I was completely surprised by the comment.

She had learned early on to keep quiet about her religion and ethnic background. I, too, sensed this lesson after witnessing the prejudice my Turkish father had suffered since moving to Alabama, Still, this bigoted reaction was sadly ironic. I had stood up in front of the class to let them know that I, as a Muslim, was not their enemy and, in fact, respected their faith because we shared our core beliefs. Yet some of my classmates had damned me to hell just the same.

The following day, I went to my English class prepared to answer more questions about my faith, but the teacher simply asked the next student to start his presentation. Nobody said anything about my continuing the presentation I had started the previous day. I was confused and disappointed at this turn of events, especially after having received such a positive reaction the day before. My English teacher, who had always been kind to me, gave me an A on my presentation, but he never explained why he hadn't let me speak again.

My family left Alabama the summer after that junior year. I returned to Tuscaloosa the following spring to see my high school friends and favorite teachers. When I visited my eleventh-grade English teacher, he finally explained what had happened after I gave my presentation. One of my classmates—likely among the group of students who had kept their ears covered—had reported the day's events to his father that evening. His father showed up in the principal's office the next morning to complain. He felt no student should have ever been allowed to speak about a topic as blasphemous as mine. This man had threatened to have the principal fired if I was ever allowed to speak again. The principal forbade my English teacher to allow my presentation to continue the next day, and he obeyed.

Looking back on this Alabama experience, I find it's a perfect example of why I am grateful for having been brought up Muslim without a Muslim community. Admittedly, life was often challenging and even frustrating for me as a young girl. I grew up with few examples to follow as I developed my own religious interpretation and practice. This lack of community denied me the ease of being surrounded by others sharing a similar lifestyle, and I frequently found myself needing to explain why I lived the way I did when nobody else seemed to live that way. Ultimately, belonging to such a small minority prevented me from becoming narrow-minded and judgmental towards others.

I learned the hard way to be open-minded about the beliefs of others. Throughout my life, others have assumed my beliefs are wrong because they are different. This painful experience has taught me not to judge other people's beliefs or assume my beliefs are the only right ones. I not only respect the beliefs of others but also seek out similarities between our faiths. I never believed my non-Muslim friends and acquaintances were wrong or dangerous for me to be around simply because of our religious differences. Had my parents instilled such rigid ideas in me, I would've had no friends at all. I may well have ended up like the classmates who'd refused to listen to my speech celebrating the similarities between our faiths.

A William & Mary Ramadan

by *Ayah H. Ibrahim*

Ayah H. Ibrahim is a graduate student at George Mason University, where she is pursuing her doctoral degree in comparative and American politics. Her research interests include minority civic engagement in pluralist states, foreign policy and interest groups, and political Islam. She received her bachelor's degree in government and Middle Eastern studies from the College of William & Mary. Born, raised, and now studying in Northern Virginia, Ayah greatly enjoys traveling her country and world. When she is not busy studying or researching, she volunteers in her local community. To relax, she paints, sketches, or creates videos and websites.

As I am about to embark on graduate school, I find myself reflecting on my undergraduate experience. It was nearly seven years ago that I attended the College of William & Mary. I had chosen a school far from both my home in Northern Virginia and any sizable Muslim community. I was afraid I would not be accepted in this unfamiliar and relatively homogenous community.

The feelings of loneliness and anxiety that haunted me as I began college were only magnified during Ramadan. This had always been a period of personal and spiritual growth for me. Without a strong support system in college, however, I worried I would lose the motivation to struggle to improve myself. I needn't have worried. My Ramadans transformed my college years from lonely to communal, full of understanding and compassion.

On the first day of Ramadan that freshman year, I rose early and ate *suhur* (early morning meal) alone. Until that day, I had always observed Ramadan with my family and as a member of a large Muslim community. Whether it was through suhur with my family or a potluck meal at the mosque, I was surrounded by others observing Ramadan. Being at college meant I would not only be missing out on the gathering of the larger community, but I would also be unable to participate in my family's small Ramadan traditions.

I felt especially lonely during suhur. I couldn't help but be envious of my siblings, who were all home for Ramadan. At college, everyone did their own thing for suhur. Some gathered junk food from vending machines, while others packed takeout boxes with pizzas, salads, or fruit from the night before. Some skipped suhur altogether, fasting without the early morning meal. Enduring lonely suhurs or reciting the dawn prayer alone simply reinforced my sense of isolation. At home, suhur and fajr were when my family all got up together to eat and pray before our day began.

In college, everything was different. From suhur to iftaar to the last prayer of the day, I observed the holy month almost entirely alone. My isolation left me conflicted. On the one hand, I felt closer to God because I believed I was overcoming the struggles of Ramadan by myself; on the other hand, my spiritual knowledge felt stagnant. I no longer strived to strengthen my

Islam because no one at college challenged or encouraged me.

Unlike my iftaars growing up—where only Muslims had participated—college offered a more diverse experience. For iftaar, I would meet up with friends—some fasting, some not—and we'd head over to The Caf. At the dining hall, we'd scatter and fill our trays. Whatever I ate first I loved, only to discover by my second serving that it was my hunger that had made the food deceptively delicious. If it hadn't been for this small group of friends who regularly broke their fast with me during my first year of Ramadan, I would have felt truly alone and without hope for better years to come. And yet I still missed the sense of community and tradition that were familiar to me.

That first year was especially frustrating. I always looked forward to Ramadan, not only for the food (few realize Ramadan is as much about the great food during iftaar as it is about abstaining from food and drink all day) but also for the company and heightened spirituality. In years past, I had focused on one goal during Ramadan: improving myself. At college, there was no one around to remind me to pray. For the first time, I didn't have to answer to anyone but God. My parents weren't going to check up on my praying. As with iftaar and suhur, I managed. I installed a computer program that calls adhan five times, marking each prayer time, and I prayed alone.

To overcome my sense of loneliness and disconnection from the larger community, I did the only thing I could think of: I organized. I helped the Muslim Students Association (MSA) shift its focus from interfaith dialoguing to outreach, which included Muslims. My Ramadan college experience would not have been complete without reaching out to other Muslims and forging a sense of community. While my first Ramadan away from family had been a relatively solitary one, my later Ramadans developed into spectacular showings of community and belonging. Being surrounded by other Muslims not only challenged me to become a better Muslim, but it also gave me the sense of ummah I had been craving. As the only Muslim girl who wore a headscarf at William & Mary, I felt a sense of relief and security in belonging to a larger whole.

During one particular week, our MSA officers—all males— made a valiant but unsuccessful effort to provide iftaar for everyone at the Arabic House.[1] I didn't expect a feast like I was accustomed to back home, but I definitely had no idea what an unforgettable breakfast we were in store for. After a daylong fast, we were served deviled eggs, Twinkies, and a juice box. Despite the paltry offerings, we felt an overwhelming sense of gratitude for their efforts and the support of the Arabic House residents who'd made cookies for our iftaar. It was a wonderful expression of the generosity embodied by everyone during Ramadan. Ultimately, this selflessness and fellowship became the foundation for the festive iftaar gatherings during my final years at college.

At William & Mary, I belonged to a small Muslim student population. With the school's lack of diversity, I had feared we would always be overlooked. During my first two years, I resented having to pay for two or three meals a day while only being able to use one during Ramadan. Many other public universities offered tailored meal plans and options for Muslims, and yet here, at the oldest public university in the United States, Muslims did not enjoy that kind of recognition.

During my third year, the MSA received some welcome assistance from an officer in Hillel, our Jewish counterpart organization. She was a senior who was well-connected with the school's administration, especially Food Services. She advised us about whom to approach with our suggestion to provide a suhur option to students who fast. This kind gesture could easily be perceived as coming from the unlikeliest of places, but to me, it

---

[1] A dorm hall, part of William & Mary's Language Housing

made perfect sense. Hillel, like the Muslim Students Association, represented a minority on campus.

With her encouragement, the MSA began working with the administration on several channels to promote inclusion across campus. We also witnessed a turning point in our relationship with other religious organizations, especially Hillel. By joining together, we accomplished far more. I hope this officer knows how much she inspired me to work in coalitions to achieve common goals.

Our MSA grew more active during my last two years. By the time I was a junior, we were holding group suhurs and iftaars on a regular basis. When I was a senior, we organized late-night trips to International House of Pancakes (IHOP), and some members organized daily before-sunrise wake-up calls. Each year, we also had a regular iftaar at a Muslim professor's home. This later became a tradition for our MSA. By sticking together through the tough times early on, we helped build a larger community based on diversity and acceptance, not simply tolerance. The term "tolerance" always indicates a level of negativity. What I witnessed, however, was genuine recognition and understanding. Classmates, friends, family, professors, and community members began to participate in our weekly iftaars at the Arabic House.

The first potluck iftaar and suhur were held at the Arabic House, which had become an unofficial gathering place for various ethnic and religious groups. Many in the dorm—some who fasted and many more who didn't—joined in. We were slowly creating our own community and Ramadan customs.

Muslim and non-Muslim students offered to cook for us. Other times, Muslim families donated dishes for the fasting students. These experiences gave me a greater feeling of inclusion and brother/sisterhood with my fellow MSAers. We all came from unique backgrounds and understandings of Islam, yet we found ourselves bound together by a growing sense of community. Simply recalling it, I feel uplifted and inspired by the way our small group of individuals from across the US came together and supported each other. Ramadan had become unlike anything I had ever known it to be, yet the values of charity, self-improvement, and community still defined the experience.

A true feeling of belonging swept over me when I realized there is more than one way to observe Ramadan. By my senior year, most of my friends had chosen to live off campus, while I remained in the dorms. My close friends took turns cooking. Maybelline's Peruvian cooking was the closest I could get to my mom's Egyptian meals, and Mona's lentil soup wasn't far off from my mother's soup. Suzie's pasta and brownies were both amazing. Tara's curry-anything was delicious, with the perfect degree of spiciness. Even though Maybelline and Tara did not fast themselves, they were anxious to support Suzie, Mona, and me during our fasting. Maybelline even regularly cooked for the weekly iftaars at the Arabic House.

With the William & Mary students and faculty as my new family away from home, I felt blessed. I would never want to change my Ramadan experiences at William & Mary. Overwhelming kindness, generosity, and camaraderie defined my college experience. Without this community, Ramadan would have remained a time of isolation for me. I feel honored to have met the people I did, especially the many who embraced, enabled, and encouraged the MSA to develop new traditions.

As my college years progressed, my sense of solitude faded completely, and I felt a growing sense of hope. This entire experience enriched me as both a human being and a Muslim. Through acts of kindness by others, I learned the importance of acceptance and compassion. Other Muslims and I not only felt accepted but sensed that we naturally belonged.

Looking back now, I still reminisce about the sense of ummah we created in that greater community at William & Mary. Even when others didn't partake in our traditions or beliefs, there was an honest effort to support our activities. The generosity of the people I befriended and their openness inspires me to be optimistic and to have faith in others.

During my first year out of college, I immersed myself in my family's beloved Ramadan traditions. All four of us kids were present at the table daily, during suhur and later as we broke our fast on my mom's delicious chicken noodle soup. Despite this joyful return to the "norm," it wasn't until I experienced a William & Mary Ramadan that I came to appreciate what this holy month truly means: self-denial, community, and charity towards all.

Soul Baring and Barrier Breaking

by Nafees Asiya Syed

Nafees Asiya Syed is currently a legislative aide for a Member of Congress and an author. Dedicated to human rights and public policy, Nafees previously worked for the U.S. House of Representatives Judiciary Committee and interned at the British Parliament and the International Criminal Tribunal for the former Yugoslavia. Her writing and research has appeared in several publications, from popular to academic outlets, including CNN.com and the International Journal of the History of Sport. *Currently, Nafees is writing a novel featuring a Muslim-American woman. A native of Georgia, Nafees graduated from Harvard University in government and medical studies. She graduated with honors, magna cum laude and Phi Beta Kappa, and received a Distinguished Senior Award from the Dean of Harvard College and the Director of the Harvard Foundation.*

About a week before the 2008 presidential elections, I was pleasantly surprised to find that my article, "Candidates Should Seek Votes of Muslim-Americans," had somehow climbed its way to the position of most-read article on *CNN.com.* My college friends informed me I had momentarily surpassed a Greek pop star as the most popular student at Harvard.

During the heat of the campaign, my identity as a writer changed. The elections unleashed a torrent of emotions within me. I was a politically minded young voter eager for a new administration that would revitalize our country's economic and foreign policy. As a college student, I was naturally concerned about post-graduation job prospects. As a human being, I was appalled by the death tolls of US soldiers, Iraqis, and Afghanis who had been thrown into a long, hard war. I was shocked and upset by how certain presidential candidates—notably Mayor Rudy Giuliani and Governor Mitt Romney—addressed Islam and Muslims. They created a dangerous political atmosphere for me as a Muslim voter. The Muslim American community had been betrayed by a party they had supported in 2000—a party that had subsequently introduced disastrous foreign and domestic policies that then alienated the Muslim community.

I had grown up respecting the importance of words. The first message of God to Muhammad was, "Read in the name of thy Lord and Cherisher, Who created" (Qur'an 96:1). I have tried all my life to adhere to that command. I have used writing to express my feelings from the time I was a child attempting my first story to now, as I write my first novel. Initially, this was how I channeled my analysis of the 2008 elections. I felt writing for Muslim readers helped the Muslim community consolidate our positions. As time went on, however, I started to wonder if this was limiting. After all, I thought, other Americans—Republicans especially—ought to know how Muslim Americans felt about the GOP rhetoric. As someone who was unaccustomed to voicing such emotions to a non-Muslim audience, I wondered whether readers would empathize with my point of view.

I wrote an op-ed arguing that the GOP ought to change its tactics and reach out to Muslim American voters. My article was published in the *Atlanta Journal-Constitution*, reaching a large and primarily Republican audience.

Within a day, hundreds of emails, letters, and Facebook messages flooded in, both praising and criticizing me. Some of the messages were terrifyingly vehement. This is an experience almost every writer expects when introducing a fresh perspective but is never fully prepared for. Some argued I was misinterpreting Rudy Giuliani's and Mitt Romney's comments, a contention I considered but still believed was false. A disappointingly large number of readers justified the political treatment of Muslims with Islamophobic opinions of their own.

Muslims and non-Muslims alike encouraged me to continue writing from this oft-ignored point of view. Whether positive or negative, the significant number of comments reflected the fact that my article had forced people to consider a different perspective. They also strengthened my conviction to communicate the Muslim-American viewpoint to other Americans. In the process, I formed valuable contacts with people who would help me get my voice heard in the future. Witnessing how a few words could affect my home community of Atlanta paved the way for me to reach out to the greater American community.

As the election neared, I realized the Republican Party was not alone in alienating Muslim Americans; the Democratic Party was also noticeably distancing itself from our community. "Muslims," "Islam," and "Arabs" were hurled as insults during the campaign as Muslim Americans watched the spectacle from the sidelines.

I remember talking to *Guardian* columnist Marc Abrahams about my desire to share how I as a Muslim-American felt about this election. He advised, "History has handed you this gift. It expires two-and-a-half weeks from now." I wrote the article, and it was accepted for publication on *CNN.com*.

I offered more personal insights in the *CNN.com* article than I had in my *Atlanta Journal-Constitution* piece. I wove in the emotional theme of a divided individual, inspired by W.E.B. DuBois's *The Souls of Black Folk*. There is something unnerving about pouring your feelings onto paper for the public to read, like letting people leaf through pages of your soul. The readership for this article was also much larger. My classmates, professors, and acquaintances were among those who would leaf through my soul and judge me.

Would Republicans resent my praise of General Powell's criticism of his party? Would Democrats be angered by my constructive criticism of the Obama campaign? In Islam, we are told to "Be maintainers of justice … though it may be against your ownselves," (Qur'an 4:135). For me, it was important to point out a wrong, even if it had been committed by my own party. The risk was worth taking. I had endured hearing one candidate use Islam as an insult while the other responded by alienating himself from the Muslim community. I, as a Muslim and as an American, had something to say about that.

I braced myself for the reactions, which turned out to be shockingly wonderful. Somehow, the article garnered more than 518,000 page views in a few days. What had captivated the readers—whether they were inspired or incensed by my words—was the association of a human story with what had become a faceless political or religious group.

Over the next couple of weeks, I saw for the first time mainstream publications such as *Newsweek* featuring articles on Muslims' feelings about the presidential election. Grateful for the hundreds of overwhelmingly positive emails, letters, and comments, I received a reassuringly small proportion of Islamophobic comments. Some also wrote in with constructive criticism that helped me broaden my own understanding. For example, one Muslim soldier pointed out that by using such hyphenated terms like "Muslim-American," we reinforce an imagined separation between Muslims and Americans. Most readers thanked me for showing them a viewpoint they had not considered, others thanked me for articulating what had been upsetting them throughout the campaign, and still others encouraged me to continue writing and even run for public office someday. While I had felt awkward about giving people a glimpse into my emotions, I realized that vulnerability is what allowed my readership to connect so strongly with the article.

There is no inherent friction between Americans and Muslims, but there are many obstacles preventing mutual understanding. As Jalal ad-Din Rumi wrote, "Your task is not to seek for love, but merely to seek and find all the barriers within yourself that you have built against it." By writing, I was removing the barriers within myself and nudging my readers to examine their own.

In this instance, I had been successful. I felt reassured that so many Americans were willing to support the Muslim–American community at a time when political parties were not. Although I knew I could not always depend on such a supportive response, it reinforced my belief that there was a need and a desire for opinions like mine to be voiced in mainstream media. Each of my articles gives me the impetus to continue writing about these political and personal issues while simultaneously pursuing a path to law and politics. It is important for me to wed my two passions—politics and writing—in my career. The need for human narratives in public discourse cannot be fulfilled without the voices of our growing Muslim community.

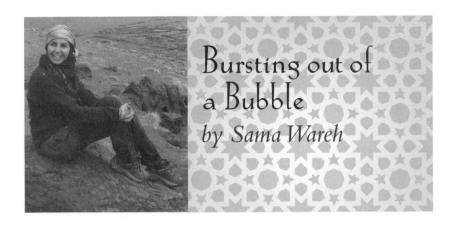

Bursting out of a Bubble
by Sama Wareh

Sama Wareh holds a master's of science in environmental stud-
ies with emphases on environmental education and communication
from California State University, Fullerton. She won the award
for Best Master's Project/Thesis for her documentary, Dwindling
Drops in the Sand, *and served as the 2009 commencement*
speaker at her alma mater. Sama has been working with the Orange
County Department of Education as a field naturalist and travel-
ing scientist. She leads outdoor science education hikes and brings
animals and education programs to schools throughout Southern
California. She sits on the YMCA Board as the environmental
program advisor. Sama is also an artist and illustrator. Her work
focuses on environmental messages, Arabic calligraphy, and abstract
design. Visit www.warehart.com to see examples of her artwork.

I wasn't prepared for the severe culture shock sixth-grade public
school would bring. Not truly understanding my surroundings
or the culture I lived in, I was naive about the average activities of American schoolchildren; contemporary practices such as

kissing in public, slang phrases, fashion standards, boyfriends and girlfriends, alcohol, drugs, and sex.

Since kindergarten, I had attended an Islamic private school. My strong Muslim upbringing strictly enforced good morals, respecting one's parents and teachers, refraining from dating or kissing in public (even between married couples), and anything even remotely considered indecent.

Both my school and home environments reinforced these values. A flat-pleated navy blue uniform draped my body, and each morning, I lined up on faded yellow painted lines to pray with my classmates. God-consciousness was instilled in me from the age of four. It was reflected every day in each action I undertook.

My private school kept true to its mission of raising us with Islamic morals. We had no Internet access. Our television set was restricted to playing G-rated movies or cartoons. We didn't have exposure to any non-Islamic influences. Although we had non-Muslim neighbors at home, they were more like grandparents to us and never caused us to question our naiveté.

When we took a test, teachers reminded the class, "God is watching." During Ramadan, we were told that even sneaking into a closet to secretly eat food was wrong because it was God's opinion that counted. The teachers explained that there were two angels, one on our left side recording our bad deeds and one on our right side recording our good deeds. On the Day of Judgment, our books would be weighed. Depending on which one was heavier, we would go to either heaven or hell.

In a way it was like having autism, where kids grow up in their own world with their own highly individualized vocabulary of understanding. All I knew was my world of unicorns, cartwheels, Friday karate lessons, Disney movies, beads, and fantasy books.

Sixth grade was like a new world to me. Not only was this my first time in public school, but I was also in a completely different neighborhood. I had no friends. I ate alone, played alone, and walked alone. Sometimes I would do cartwheels across the asphalt on my way to my next class. I was blessed in my isolation—it helped me preserve who I was. My exposure to the dazzling, over-glorified world of public school only fortified the strength of character with which I was raised.

One day, an incident occurred that would forever redefine and shape me. A gang of girls sat next to me at my pale green lunch table. They were everything a girl trying to be popular would aspire to be. My brown-bag lunch looked humble beside their school lunch trays. The pack moved in, with the lead wolf speaking on the group's behalf. They marched me out to the soccer field, stationing me in front of a blonde-haired boy.

"Okay, Sama, this is Daaron, and you have to kiss him on the lips." I looked straight at Daaron. His eyes were closed, and his lips were pursed. My heart sank into my feet. I knew kissing a boy on the lips would be blasphemous in the eyes of God and my parents. I couldn't bring myself to say no, but I never expected to have the courage to do what came next.

"Go on, kiss him on the lips! You want to be in our group, right?" the wolf leader chanted. I looked at them, my eyes betraying my fragile emotions. Suddenly, all of my angry energy and frustration rushed into my fist, which flew from my side into Daaron's right shoulder. He clutched his arm in agony as I fled the soccer field, shouting "Sorry!" When I tried apologizing to him the next day, he yelled, "Get away from me, you bully!"

This had not been my first encounter with a guy who had a crush on me. Although I made no effort to attract guys, sixth grade turned me into walking prey. My loneliness seemed to make it easier for guys to approach me. When they asked me out, I had no idea what it meant.

"Hey, you want to go out with me?" a boy asked one time. I looked at him like he was the most brain-deficient person on the planet and explained that we were already outside.

"No, I mean, you want to be my girlfriend?" he clarified. That didn't go too well, either.

I was no longer inside my private school cocoon, where girls were terrified of cooties from touching a boy's hand. I was not used to a system where people looked to fashion, music, sex, and the latest trends instead of to God. Lying in bed that evening, I stared up at the ceiling. I knew then, as I know now, that life is about making choices. I wanted to make good ones.

I am proud of the choice I made on the soccer field that day. Not giving into peer pressure helped me reaffirm my faith and values. This decision to stay true to what I want rather than what others want increased my self-esteem and ability to stand up to social pressure.

After sixth grade, I continued to make positive choices that helped shape me into a leader. I wasn't always leading others, but I was always my own leader. One of these choices involved starting to wear a headscarf in seventh grade. I continued this practice into eighth grade, feeling reinvented as I walked the halls of my school. I had made up my mind. I prided myself on being the different one. I didn't care if nobody wanted to hang out with me because I wore a scarf. It helped me find people who were true friends.

With that attitude, I carried on through high school, bringing a scarf, long sleeves, and a bright outlook to the various athletic teams I served on. I realized it was a waste of time to worry about what people thought of me. It only brings you down and detracts from your creative energy.

Sometimes my eyes would be drawn to something that appeared glamorous. Like a raven fixated on shiny jewelry, I would stare and ponder before snapping out of it and realizing it contained no substance. I would spend my time drawing during class and recess, finishing my homework over lunch and practicing art when I got home. I considered television a waste of time, even though not watching it made me clueless about what everyone was gossiping about the next day.

This philosophy had emerged from much inner contemplation and the sense of discontent I felt when I wasted time. I understood that appearances and social norms didn't warrant real value. I saw how social pressures often distracted people from being themselves and discovering their true potential. Time was of the essence, and sculpting myself into an artist was important to me.

While my family provided the supportive environment I needed to be an artist, my thought process was nurtured by a couple of significant influences in my life. The first was my best friend, Ferdaus. We shared the same beliefs, and together, we discussed our projects and imagined how to better ourselves.

My sister was the second influence. The summer following high school graduation, I spent two months visiting her in Salt Lake City, Utah. We both picked talents to hone and literary works to study together. The mother of four kids and an expert at conquering her schedule, my sister inspired me to spend my time wisely.

Ferdaus and my sister formed a support system for me. We exchanged ideas and kept each other motivated. By the time I entered college, I was driven by a passion to pursue personal growth at every opportunity.

That principle served me well both during and after college. Today, I run my own art business and lead nature trail hikes in California. I've been featured on the cover of *Yahoo!* with a surfboard in hand, and I am currently working with the United Nations on a documentary about Syria's water crisis.

The bubble of private school helped me preserve my morals. Years later, seeing myself on *Yahoo!* cloaked in a full scarf and body suit reinforced my awareness of the modesty I have come to cherish. Sticking to your morals can lead to success and recognition, while caring too much about others' expectations diverts us from discovering who we truly are.

The rawness of public school taught me that assimilation did not necessarily mean compromise. While I was filming my documentary and being interrogated by Syrian secret service, my instinct to run kicked in as vividly as my instinct to punch the sixth-grade boy in the arm. I am street-savvy and aware of my surroundings thanks to my public school experience, but I am also graceful and in tune with my faith because of my formative years in Islamic school. Ultimately, I discovered that navigating both public and private schools taught me how to navigate my public and private *selves*.

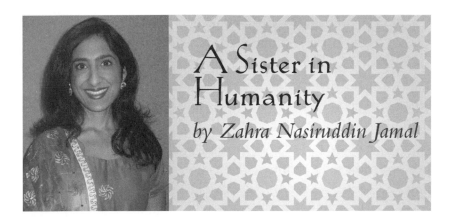

A Sister in Humanity

by Zahra Nasiruddin Jamal

Zahra Nasiruddin Jamal is a passionate community leader. Appointed to two boards by His Highness the Aga Khan, she oversees social welfare and religious education initiatives in the United States. Zahra has consulted on conflict resolution and women's rights projects for the United Nations and other organizations. She's met with the US ambassador to the Netherlands and Muslim leaders to increase Muslim civic participation in Western countries. Designer of the Aspen Institute's Muslim Philanthropy Project, Zahra is assistant professor and director of the Central Asia and International Development Program at Michigan State University. She researches gender, transnationalism, and civic engagement among Muslims in North America as well as South and Central Asia. Previously an award-winning anthropology lecturer at Harvard and MIT, Zahra held the Javits, Mellon, Weatherhead, and Hearst Fellowships. Zahra completed her PhD in anthropology and Middle Eastern studies at Harvard and earned degrees in Islamic studies and Slavic studies from Rice University.

"No, she can't enter!" the visa officer shouted. I was standing in the vestibule of the Dushanbe airport, waiting to be granted entry into Tajikistan shortly after 9/11. Another South Asian Canadian Muslim woman, also named Zahra, had sailed through. The combination of my American nationality, Muslim-sounding name, and South Asian ethnicity caused grave concern among the airport officials. They had been influenced by the media's questioning of American Muslims' trustworthiness, its portrayals of the so-called Axis of Evil, and tensions surrounding the India-Pakistan race to employ nuclear energy. Politics, history, religion, and fear intertwined at that moment to mark me as "the other."

As a South Asian American Muslim woman born and raised in New York, I celebrate pluralism. This ethic underpins both the Islamic and the American traditions that shape my identity. Pluralism also motivates me as a social anthropologist. It requires a willingness to accept and learn from "the other," to see difference as strength rather than as weakness. Yet I have repeatedly encountered one specific lesson during my experiences in the US and abroad: while our world is pluralistic in makeup, it is not pluralistic in mindset. Despite how we define ourselves, others often redefine us according to their beliefs while denigrating our differences.

The values espoused in the Qur'an—of equality, caring for the marginalized, valuing human life and its diversity—resonate deeply with the values in the US Constitution. Many wrongly assume the Qur'an depicts Muslim women as inferior to men and think Muslim women must be "saved" by Western women. I counter such views by *living* the rights and equalities accorded me as a Muslim woman based on many interpretations of Islam and the Shia Nizari Ismailism[1] tradition.

---

[1] A branch of Shia Islam led by an Aga Khan, a hereditary title given to the imam who leads this community. Their current Aga Khan is Prince Karīm al-Hussainī, who assumed this title in 1957 at the age of twenty.

In the mid-twentieth century, Sir Sultan Muhammad Shah Aga Khan III, forty-eighth imam of the Ismaili Muslims, remarked, "My ancestor, the holy prophet [Muhammad], encouraged the evolution of all legitimate freedom and legitimate equality between men and women." Surprisingly, he encouraged followers who could only afford to educate one child to choose the daughter, because to educate a woman means to educate a family.

Inspired by this statement, I have sought educational excellence, professional development, and social and financial independence. My right to decide my own future is encouraged by Islam, as well as by the American values of equality and social justice.

Practicing the ethics common to both traditions makes this balance easy—precisely because there is no contradiction in being Muslim and American. Yet growing up as a Muslim woman in America was not always easy. My childhood was marked by both racial bigotry and broadminded pluralism. Some see difference as an opportunity to discriminate, while others see it as an opportunity to learn.

I grew up in the 1980s. I remember my best friend in elementary school telling me one day, "My mom says we can't be friends anymore because you're not white." Another time, the neighborhood boys my brother and I used to play basketball with started beating my brother on our front porch for being "too brown."

Yet I also remember my elementary and middle school teachers asking me to teach my classmates about life as a Muslim, since our textbooks did not cover much more than trite formulae such as the "Five Pillars." Many of my classmates were eager to learn about the Qur'an, Eid festivals, and Ramadan. Some students and teachers even tried fasting during Ramadan.

These latter experiences—of others viewing difference as enriching rather than as dividing—give me hope. It is during these moments that we see "the other" not as a liability but as a vital member of our global village.

As an anthropologist, I seek to understand others' lives in their own terms, not in the terms that have been imposed upon them. During my research ventures, however, I have not always been accorded that same respect. Some are quick to essentialize me, often viewing difference myopically.

In America, I have observed that some individuals have not been exposed to the diversity of interpretations and practices within Islam. While volunteering with an interfaith organization in Texas, I was caught off-guard by my supervisor one day. She asked casually, "You're not *really* Muslim, right?" She had wrongly assumed that all practicing Muslim women wear a veil and that anyone who did not must be secular and Westernized. My supervisor was fascinated to learn that many interpretations of Islam, including my own, do not require or even encourage veiling.

A couple of years later, I traveled to Pakistan. Visiting relatives in Karachi had been exciting to me as a child. Everyone wanted to practice their English with my brother and me, hear about our lives in America, and enjoy the gifts and treats we brought from the "Promised Land."

By 2005, being American had become a liability. Pakistanis warned me not to register with the American Embassy or tell local shopkeepers I was American. With mild trepidation, I watched anti-Western protesters on the streets and read about more protests in the local newspapers. I fashioned my grandmother's long scarf, her *dupata* into a *burqa* cloak to cover my jeans and t-shirt, shielding myself from peoples' inquisitive stares and prodding hands as I walked through crowded markets and into male-dominated Internet cafés.

A few days later, I was subjected to reverse-essentializing on my return flight from Karachi to JFK on Pakistani International Airlines. While I was "too American" in Pakistan, I was now "too Muslim" during our layover in Manchester, UK, where we were hoarded like animals through extra security checkpoints and body searches. One passenger called it "the 'Paki' treatment," which often occurs at European checkpoints, where Muslim and Pakistani identities are conflated.

Both Islam and America grant me freedom and equality. Yet, during times of political and social tensions, my Muslim identity has been essentialized in the Western world, while my American identity has been essentialized in the Muslim world. And that is not very liberating. It signals a larger need for Western and Muslim societies to earnestly seek to understand "the other" in her own terms. When we do, we see that she is our neighbor, a fellow human, with an equally valid way of life. She is neither our enemy nor our "cause." She is our sister in humanity. Just as I am yours.

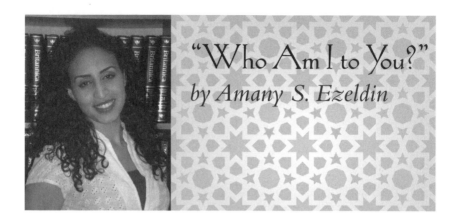

"Who Am I to You?"
by Amany S. Ezeldin

Amany S. Ezeldin is an attorney at Life Span Center for Legal Services and Advocacy, where she works with immigrant victims of domestic violence and sexual assault. She is also an adjunct professor of human rights at Columbia College. When she is not working, Amany enjoys hiking, biking, attending Chicago's outdoor summer festivals and concerts, performing in theatrical productions, reading, and laughing. The middle child of a family with five children, Amany was born and raised in Chicago to her Egyptian parents, who immigrated to the United States in the 1970s.

I didn't realize I was a "_____-American" (pick one: Muslim, Arab, Egyptian, Other) until high school. I had certainly received inquiries about my identity, but I had no idea what taking on these identities meant to me and the people around me.

Growing up in a middle class Chicago suburb, I looked different from my peers. Despite the fact that my hair could be described as a fro-mullet, I somehow didn't catch on that I actually *was* different—even when the neighborhood kids acted puzzled at seeing my mother performing ritual Islamic prayers.

I now realize others had identified me as different early in my life. I walked around with my fro-mullet and didn't eat lunch in the cafeteria during Ramadan, but I was oblivious that others had noticed or even found these differences odd.

Growing up, I was often confronted with my differences—I just didn't understand what was going on. The earliest occurrence was in first grade. I was too innocent to realize I was being asked to self-identify. I was taking a standardized test that required me to fill in bubbles corresponding to my name, date of birth, and ethnicity. My teacher, with what I now understand was a look of distress, called me into the hallway.

"Where are you from? What are you?" the teacher asked. My tiny six-year-old self failed to comprehend the enormity of that moment. These are huge, loaded questions. People spend years searching for their identity. Even when I am asked these questions now, I find them difficult to answer. Sometimes I alter my response based on the audience. I usually stutter an answer, unsure whether the person wants to know which suburb I am from or why I look the way I do. It becomes a significant undertaking to self-identify when there are so many facets to your identity.

Although I can't exactly remember, I imagine I told my first-grade teacher I was Egyptian. Guided by her teacher's manual, she told me to choose "White/Caucasian." And that was good enough for me, especially since my classmates were choosing the same bubble. That is probably why the little olive-skinned girl with a fro-mullet who brought peanut-butter-and-jelly sandwiches in pita bread walked around thinking she was white for so long. I knew I was Muslim and I knew I was Egyptian and I knew none of the other kids were either one of those, but at the time, none of this meant anything to my self-identity.

Although I spent the early years of my life in a middle-class, cookie-cutter subdivision in Chicago, I had also spent many summers in the agricultural town in Egypt where my parents had emigrated from. Twenty years ago, life in that Egyptian town was starkly different from my life in the United States. Water and electricity were regularly cut off, natural gas for ovens and heating water had not yet been installed, most families didn't have a phone in their house, and livestock was often driven through the town. While we had virtually no family in the US, Egypt teemed with Arabic-speaking relatives whose customs were strange compared with those of our American family friends. Their lifestyle couldn't have been more different.

I successfully compartmentalized these two lives: my long, hot summers in a small Egyptian town and my academic years in American suburbia. Everything changed, however, when I lived in Egypt for two years while attending high school with other Egyptians. Suddenly, among all of these other Egyptians, I was not a minority. Ironically, this was the first time I had ever realized that back in America, I *was* a minority.

Almost everyone in Egypt was like me. My classmates were all Egyptian, which meant the majority of them were Muslim, spoke Arabic at home, and ate pita bread, which wasn't exotic to them and was just, well, bread. I was distressed because even though I was surrounded by people who looked like me and spoke Arabic like me and practiced the same religion as me, I suddenly felt very different. What a prank to discover that once I was surrounded by "my people," I felt different. I really only related to the other classmates who were also American or whose families had repatriated back to Egypt from Europe. It seemed I wasn't truly like everyone else—either in America *or* Egypt.

When I returned to the United States, I lived in a community comprising over 50 percent immigrants or first-generation immigrants. It wasn't until I was surrounded by other "_____-Americans" that I finally felt like everyone else. I learned that I am a "_____-American," and I need both parts to define myself.

The plurality of my identity is what defines me. It's hard

to pinpoint exactly how much of one identity I favor. I hear this dilemma described all the time by people who are also "_____-American." There is often a struggle to fit into one group over the other. Many people say they are many things, and they cannot disassociate themselves from one or more of their identities.

Today, I take comfort in my ability to be many things. Who wants to be constrained by one stereotype? And when someone asks, "What are you?", do they really want to hear me say, "I am a far-left–leaning liberal, a Muslim, an Egyptian, a Chicagoan, a woman, an African, a Middle Easterner, an Arab, a first-generation American, and a lawyer?"

I can't really define myself without all of those labels. Now, when I am asked to identify my race or ethnicity, I color in the bubble for "Other." And I like that. I like the ambiguity of my identity and the freedom to define myself however I choose.

Truth Is Not Always Self-Evident
by Rabea Chaudhry

Rabea Chaudhry is an artist, attorney, and writer living in the Bay Area with her husband, Farukh Rashid, and their beautiful daughter, Summer. Her artwork has been displayed all over the country, including Berkeley's University Press Cafe and the New Orleans Museum of African American Art and History. Her writing has been published in the Journal of Islamic Near Eastern Law *and* The National *as well as at* Altmuslimah.com.

The summer after 9/11, I was lucky enough to attend a lecture series by Dr. Umar Faruq Abd-Allah titled "Islam in America." Shedding light on Islam's longtime presence in America and Muslims' historic respect for native cultures, Dr. Umar passed on one particular piece of wisdom that has stuck with me for years. He compared Islam to the clear water of a river that takes on the colors, forms, and textures of whatever stones it runs above. Even now—after being married for six years, completing law school, delving into the professional world, and starting a family—I continue to find great meaning in those words.

Well into my early twenties, I took the truth of Islam for granted. I believed it to be self-evident. Although I have always considered Islam an integral part of my identity, I had reduced it to simplistic mandates, truly ignorant of the rich intellectual heritage of traditional Islam. I now believe the myriad manifestations of Islam that embrace cultural nuances and practices—from the Islam of Africa to the Islam of Malaysia—have all been possible because of the understanding of earlier Muslims that, although Islam was designed to bring universal principles to the world, it was also meant to encourage and promulgate diversity.

Unfortunately, the Islam I knew for most of my life—the Islam that is becoming increasingly pervasive in the contemporary world—was resolute and dogmatic rather than expansive and amenable. Two telling examples of how close-minded my understanding of Islam was are the manner in which I first judged the religiosity of the man who is now my husband, Farukh Rashid, and my initial reaction to the Socratic method's use in law school.

I met Farukh when I was a junior in college. Instantly smitten by his pleasant disposition and infectious personality, I melted into giggles and flushed cheeks during my awkward interactions with him. I soon decided I wanted to marry Farukh. In my mind, he was perfectly nice, wonderfully sociable, and undeniably gracious and kind. I realized he was a great catch and one I wanted for myself.

There was just one hurdle. I didn't think Farukh took Islam as seriously as I did. I had naively determined his religiosity was not on the same level as mine. At the time, I had believed outward manifestations could accurately convey one's religiosity. Praying extra prayers at our campus Friday prayer service while the rest of the students greeted each other and hurried off to lunch, constantly keeping one's fingers busy with prayer beads, carrying around religious books for everyone to see what was on the weekly reading list—these were all indicators I used to measure one's relationship with God (and all practices I proudly adhered to at the time). I was too busy stroking my ego and seeking others' approval to recognize traditional Islam's admonition that arrogance is a state of the diseased heart.

I had grown up in an environment in which external rituals were seen as clear indicators of one's devotion to Islam and God Himself. A woman wearing a scarf was perceived as being closer to God and a more sincere believer than a woman without one. A man wearing a beard in the tradition of the Prophet Muhammad was recognized as being more religious and was assumed to be more knowledgeable about Islam than a clean-shaven man. These distinctions are arbitrary, I see now, but at the time, I did not question the fallacy that one's purity of heart could be measured by a predetermined set of external realities.

Despite my concerns that Farukh was not as religious as I was, my heart inclined more toward him, and I eventually called Farukh to discuss my obvious attraction to him. I was elated when he expressed a similar attraction. We began getting to know each other under the auspices of a potential marriage. In keeping with my arrogance, I was quick to relay to him my disapproval of his "lax" devotion of the religion. He was wise enough to respond with softness and flexibility.

Although I could only see one way of being a Muslim, Farukh knew there are many ways to be a servant of God. He soon acquiesced to my demands that he manifest his Islam by exhibiting the outward ostentation I had come to believe was true religiosity. To appease me, he began taking notes at our weekly religious lectures rather than just listening attentively. He started carrying around prayer beads, and he even began performing voluntary prayers at our Friday gatherings instead of waiting until he got home that afternoon. Steadily, our attraction to one another developed into a deep love, and we were married in October 2004. I am still haunted by the awareness that my own narrow-minded rigidity could have sabotaged our relationship—if not for Farukh's gentleness and versatility.

I had lacked the ability to see my husband's commitment to God in his acts of kindness and compassion, whether it be listening patiently for hours as a friend shared his problems or serving as a perpetual host to the many young Muslim men who found comfort and hospitality in his apartment. It took some time for me to realize the very things that had attracted me to Farukh in the first place—the sincerity of his character, his generosity, and his gentility—were all manifestations of his devotion to Islam. Although he did not publicize his love for God through pompous displays of religiosity, he was and is truly in love with God and committed to His service.

Watching my husband bravely confront life and its trials has slowly opened my eyes to what is lacking in my relationship with God and my understanding of His vast mercy. My limited perception of truth and my dogmatic insistence that Islam take one specific form were the consequences of an undeveloped understanding of Islam's ubiquity.

Islam is not a rigid ethos that forces conformity. Like a stream of fresh water, it is unresisting and pliable, flowing through the chasms of our inner being and enabling us to use our individuality in the most noble of ways. Although there are basic tenets of belief all Muslims must adhere to, Islam is also a means by which believers enjoy the potential to explore their own unique gifts, each contributing to the world in his or her own unique way.

My time in law school also opened my eyes to the complexity and vastness of Islam. When I first started law school in fall 2005, I was terrified to use the Socratic method. During class, we were expected to engage in open discussion of the strengths and weaknesses of each side of an issue. I was suddenly swimming in a world of gray, and the binaries of black and white, of truth and falsehood, suddenly evaded me.

"How can it be moral to argue both for *and* against a position?" I used to worry. "Is it the Islamic thing to do?" So outraged was I by the nature of our class discussions that I felt compelled to share my feelings with a close friend. I remember complaining to her, "We're supposed to argue *both* sides of any issue!"

Equally disgusted, she responded, "I cannot even imagine what that would be like!" We were too naive to realize truth is not always self-evident. For, as Socrates once proclaimed, "The highest form of Human Excellence is to question oneself and others."

Both my friend and I had relied on simplistic truths and derived comfort from a world in which truth and our understanding of Islam were absolute. Our constructions of a codified Islam were sadly in line with how Islam had been represented to us by fellow Muslims. We took others' inflexible definitions of Islam for granted without examining their credentials. Just as one cannot become a trained artist without years of practice, one cannot speak authoritatively about Islam without the proper training and knowledge.

Unfortunately, we did not realize our understanding of Islam was a far cry from the mercy and expansiveness of traditional Islam, which has been severely eroded by the fall of the Muslim Empire, the subsequent destruction of traditional schools of knowledge, and the political agendas that currently influence the dissemination and interpretation of Islam. These realities have contributed to the usurping of traditional Islam's intellectual diversity.

As contemporary Muslims, we must reacquaint ourselves with the beauty, compassion, and breadth of traditional Islam to successfully articulate the place of Islam in our postmodern world. We must begin by deriving our knowledge of Islam from qualified traditional Islamic scholars.

A dear friend of my sister's recently spent a year in Syria studying Islam under one such scholar. When she returned, I was anxious that she would no longer be the same person because of her newfound knowledge of Islam. I feared she would judge me in the same way I had judged Farukh. Much to my surprise, she did not judge me at all. I worried my boisterous personality would offend her or my clothes would be too form-fitting for her sensibilities—or that she would interpret the speed of my prayers as insincerity in my devotion. When I later confessed these concerns to her, she smiled and said, "My teacher taught me that knowledge is mercy. The more you know, the less you will judge others." I can think of no better representation of the spirit of truth and of Islam than this statement. The more we study and learn about Islam, the more we will realize how little we know about truth—and the less we will insist on imposing rigid delineations of Islam on others and ourselves.

The many lessons I have learned about the complexities of truth continue to inform my identity as a Muslim and my developing understanding of Islam. I now believe truth is a constant intellectual and spiritual engagement with our surroundings, the people we come into contact with, and the challenges we face individually and collectively. The river Dr. Abd-Allah had described during his summer 2002 lecture was the river of Islam. As the great sage Lao-Tzu says in the seventy-eighth verse of his work *Tao Te Ching*, "Water is the softest and most yielding substance. Yet nothing is better than water for overcoming the hard and rigid, because nothing can compete with it."[1]

The river of Islam is soft and malleable; it is neither rigid nor harsh and unyielding. The colors of this river vary depending on time, place, and the positioning of the river's beholder, but the purity and flexibility of this river will remain constant, continually providing believers and humanity with respite from the hardships of this world.

---

[1] Tormond Byrn's translation.

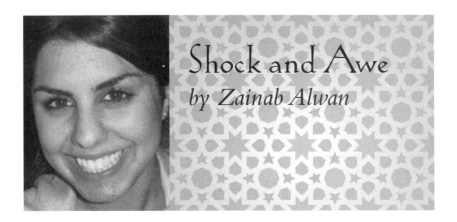

Shock and Awe
by Zainab Alwan

Zainab Alwan attends Case Western Reserve University School of Law, where she is focusing on immigration law. She graduated from the University of Rochester with a bachelor's degree in religious studies and a biology minor. Zainab is heavily involved in interfaith mediation and dispute resolution work. She cofounded the Muslim-Jewish Dialogue program at the University of Rochester, served as an outreach education and training intern for the Interfaith Youth Core, was a counselor at an international peace camp called Seeds of Peace, and worked as a law clerk with Council on American-Islamic Relations (CAIR) in Chicago. As president of the International Law Society, Zainab helped raise over $600 for the Invisible Children Foundation and over $2,000 for earthquake victims in Haiti. She enjoys spending her spare time with family and friends or running.

I had woken up late again and was racing to get dressed for another day at school. As I brushed my teeth, I heard the soothing voice of an imam coming from my mother's tape player. Like every other morning, my mother was listening to a Qur'an recitation. A few minutes later, I flew down the stairs, yelled "Love you, Mama!", and slammed the door behind me. Hopping into my beloved Toyota Camry, I excitedly drove down the road to my high school. (Yes, I was one of those students who is always enthusiastic about school.)

It was March 21, 2003, the day the US government had unleashed a torrential downpour of "smart bombs" on the city of Baghdad—otherwise known as the Shock and Awe campaign. While my Iraqi family members were huddled in their Baghdad homes waiting for the sky to calm, I was changing into my gym clothes and chatting with my two best friends, Gretchen and Bridget, before class. What was on today's schedule? Fly fishing. Ah yes, the wonders of fly fishing! Today we were learning how to make bait.

Soon, it was time for lunch. I noticed the television was on in the cafeteria. It looked like something major was happening in Iraq, but I knew if I looked too closely, I ran the risk of becoming upset. I turned my back to the TV and resumed talking with my friends.

Reaching for an apple, I stole a glance at the television screen. Flashes of bright light illuminated the Iraqi sky, now an odd shade of green. I quickly turned away again. How could the reality of the faraway war touch me when it was a beautiful March day in New York? The skies were blue and it was Friday, the first day of spring. Everyone was looking forward to the weekend. Yet as I sat in the cafeteria gossiping and crunching on my apple, my uncle sat crouching in Baghdad, clutching his family in terror.

I was oblivious to the bombardment and intended to keep it that way. Chemistry was next. This was always an exciting class as it gave me a chance to fine-tune my multitasking skills. Each day, I attempted to pay attention to Mrs. Taylor while simultaneously writing notes to Gretchen.

Today was a bit different, however. Mrs. Taylor ended class early and asked if we wanted to watch the news, since some sort of campaign was going on in Iraq. I became more engrossed in my note-writing, almost forgetting the television until a loud eruption blared from the speakers. My head jolted up, and my eyes met a horrific display of military power. The Iraqi sky was filled with smoke and, as my friend later described, it looked like malfunctioning fireworks were exploding in every direction.

Millions of thoughts flashed through my mind. I remembered the time I had visited Iraq in 1998 and had finally met my cousin Zainab—and how incredibly happy she was as I handed her a ten-dollar bill. Where was she now? Was her family still living in that home the size of my bedroom? Surely, their roof could not withstand this military bombardment.

Then my aunt's voice floated through my head as she explained what the Persian Gulf War was like: "You could not do anything but wait, ya Zainab. You sat with your family, everyone pushed together, and then the house lit up and the ground trembled, and everyone looked at each other and wondered who had been hit this time."

I couldn't fathom what it felt like to be in Baghdad at that moment. As I sat in class, watching the city of Baghdad crumble, I felt sick to my stomach, I felt selfish for being so safe, and I felt alone in this room filled with classmates who could not possibly appreciate the magnitude of what we were witnessing.

I sat praying for my family, knowing that even if they survived this war, the aftermath would be just as devastating. Cancer rates had been increasing steadily since the Iran-Iraq War (1980–1988), the Persian Gulf War (1990–1991), and the ten-year embargo. The number of victims would only continue to rise. Security would be nonexistent. And a country once known for its advanced universities would be scrambling to provide its children with pencils and sheets of paper.

I knew this was all true, but I had not allowed myself to acknowledge the reality of the war until that moment. I could feel tears slowly welling up. Mrs. Taylor approached me, asking if I was all right. I mumbled something about being fine and walked out of the room. The walk turned into a jog and then into a sprint as I rushed into a bathroom stall and began sobbing.

After I composed myself, I opened the door and was greeted by three of my teachers, each peering in with a look of extreme concern. I knew none of them knew how to approach me. Here I was, a sixteen-year-old Iraqi American Muslim girl unable to reach out to the family she had just watched her government pummel with bombs. My teachers offered their condolences and asked if I needed help. I smiled and pretended everything was just fine. Everyone knew my response wasn't sincere, but I felt the barrier between us was too thick for either side to break through. I was different; I just had to accept that.

I left the group of teachers feeling alone and overwhelmed. A moment later, I heard someone rushing after me. I turned to see Mrs. Taylor. She grabbed me in a tight motherly hug and said, "Zainab, I'm so sorry this happened to your family. My son might get sent over to Iraq. We are all hoping this ends soon. Zainab, we're in this together."

I was shocked and moved by her sincerity—she actually *did* care about my family. And I was further shocked by my own complete disregard for those around me. My fellow classmates may not have fully understood how difficult it was to have family in a war-torn country, but I wasn't even giving them a chance to push through that barrier.

I decided to be more open with my friends. I wanted to understand their struggles and have them understand my family's in return. I knew if my friends could even slightly grasp the magnitude of the war, we could work together to raise awareness and help civilians. If I couldn't physically reach my family, the least I could do was explain their situation. After one of these discussions, some friends and I decided to hold a bake sale at school, with proceeds going to displaced Iraqi children. Two or three students glared at our table, but the majority jumped at the opportunity to donate. It was incredible to see how a few conversations could put a face to the war and motivate others to help the civilians.

My fellow classmates could have gone on with their lives, not giving the war a second thought. Instead, they asked if my family was okay. They asked if I was okay. They voiced their support for my family and me at a time when they could have easily ignored the war taking place thousands of miles away from them.

Talking about my family in Iraq—telling my friends how scared I was and, more importantly, how scared *my family* was— helped my friends and me understand each other more deeply. I stopped feeling different from everyone else and wasn't constantly on the defense. The few times a student did make a derogatory or insensitive comment, a friend or teacher would step up to defend Iraqis before I could even say a word.

A few weeks after Shock and Awe, my history teacher asked if anyone had any solutions to the war. One of the students yelled out, "Let's just bomb them all!" An awkward silence filled the room, and before I could even gather my thoughts to speak, the entire class was in an uproar. My teacher turned to me and said, "Zainab, you can hit him, and if you don't want to, I will." I found all of this support in a small farm town in New York, where most of the students and teachers had never been friends with a Muslim until I stepped into the classroom.

As a teen, I thought in terms of labels—I am an Iraqi American Muslim, and you are an Irish Catholic American. Labels became fixed boxes around my personality. I thought if our labels were different, we could only connect on a minimal level. As I reflect on that time, I realize I almost slipped into a "victim mentality" of thinking nobody could understand me. After 9/11, I had many conversations with fellow Muslim friends who exhibited this way of thinking. They felt alone and uncomfortable in a country where they thought the majority neither understood nor cared to understand their struggle.

Mrs. Taylor quashed that restrictive belief in me. I now see labels as stagnant words society has used to describe incredibly intricate cultures, religions, and nationalities. Our differing labels are not barriers with warning signs of incompatibility. Rather, they are opportunities for us to learn from one another and grow as human beings.

After high school, I decided to become more involved in my community. I began doing interfaith work, partly to prove to myself that labels could not stand in the way of my fully connecting with others. I became actively involved with the Muslim Students Association (MSA) and worked hard to erase stereotypes and misconceptions.

Experience has taught me to never assume that others cannot or do not want to understand. At the core of it all, we have a set of common values: compassion, hope, and hospitality. The only way we can hope to overcome violent misunderstandings is by building on these commonalities and working together to realize shared goals.

On March 21, 2003, Mrs. Taylor showed me compassion, profoundly altering my approach to life with a two-minute conversation.

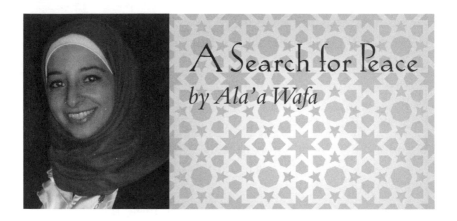

A Search for Peace
by Ala'a Wafa

Ala'a Wafa graduated from the University of Wisconsin–Madison with a bachelor's degree in international studies and political science. After college, she moved to the East Coast, where she spent two years working on Capitol Hill in Washington, DC. Ala'a then decided to pursue a law degree from Michigan State University (MSU) College of Law, graduating in May 2010 with an international and comparative law concentration. During law school, she served as an editor for MSU's Journal of International Law; competed in a moot arbitration competition in Vienna, Austria; and published an article in a legal journal. Ala'a hopes to specialize in US–Middle East relations, with special emphasis on the Palestinian-Israeli conflict. She is inspired by her grandparents' struggles as Palestinian refugees and their dream to see a peaceful resolution in their lifetime. In her free time, Ala'a enjoys photography, painting, traveling, and spending time with family and friends.

Growing up in southern Indiana, I wanted to feel I could be both American and Muslim simultaneously. My classmates, however, made me feel otherwise. I wondered why my name was different and why my mom wore a headscarf when no one else's mom did. It wasn't until middle school that I finally found sanctuary in the companionship of a religiously diverse group of friends.

This inseparable group comprised two Christians, two Jews, a Catholic, an atheist, and me. Between our conversations about music, clothes, and movies, the seven of us engaged in atypical conversations about religion, beliefs, and practices. My friends helped me strike a balance between the American and Muslim parts to my identity. I really *could* be a Palestinian, a Muslim, and an American at the same time. Years later, I put the valuable lessons they taught me into practice as I began pursuing my career.

Starting off as an intern in a senator's office on Capitol Hill, I was soon promoted to full-time Senate employee. In spite of the growing fear, resentment, and discrimination Muslim Americans have faced since September 11, I became the first known hijab-wearing Muslim to work as a paid staffer in the Senate. I was a Palestinian Muslim American female working for a Jewish American male senator. The experience helped me find my place as a Muslim American. My religion was never an issue with the staff or the senator. No one ever asked me why I had started wearing a headscarf while not having worn one as an intern the year before, nor did this development stop them from offering me a job. On the contrary, the staff seemed to appreciate the new perspective I brought to the office.

Inspired by the senator's passionate efforts to fight injustice around the world, I left The Hill determined to work towards a peaceful resolution to the Palestinian-Israeli conflict. As a grandchild of Palestinians expelled in 1948, I have always held this cause dear to my heart.

Both American ideals and Islam preach the importance of speaking out against injustice. I had to come to terms with the fact that my country was sending aid and ammunition to a country that was making the lives of my family unbearable. Yet my country was also giving me the opportunity to learn, work, and become empowered to make a difference in the world. Every country makes mistakes, but running away is not the solution. As a Muslim American, I felt compelled to better my country by improving its foreign policy.

The summer after my first year of law school, I left for Jerusalem with a program designed to work towards Palestinian-Israeli peace. Led by an Israeli Jew, twenty-five Americans and Europeans of various beliefs joined together to understand all sides of the conflict. Our hope was to one day use that knowledge as a tool in formulating a peaceful resolution.

During orientation at a Palestinian refugee camp in Bethlehem, we met to reflect on our feelings and thoughts after the first two days. A white American girl from the Midwest was the first to share. As she formed her words, tears began to fall. She explained that her parents had not wanted her to come because they were afraid she would get hurt in Palestinian areas, and their lack of support saddened her. She talked about her recognition that Palestinians and Muslims are not dangerous people, articulating that this is not a Palestinian issue, not an Arab issue, but a humanitarian issue for the whole world to care about. Her statement brought me to tears.

Two days later, we moved to a Jewish kibbutz in northern Israel, where some of us embarked on an excursion with a couple of Israeli locals. Both serving in the army, the Israelis got into a heated debate about whether Muslims were bad people. The midwestern girl whose words had moved me so deeply two nights earlier courageously spoke up on behalf of Muslims. Getting to know each other on a personal level was all it took for the two of us to see each other as fellow human beings and beyond that, as friends.

During a visit to Tel Aviv a few weeks later, some students and I attended a protest by local Israelis against their government's occupation of Palestine. A nice-looking woman—who must have assumed I was Jewish because my headscarf was tied into a bun—stopped to tell me, "I cannot understand how you, an Orthodox Jew, could possibly stand with those other Jews in support of the dirty Arabs." She continued, "You're siding with the enemy!" Confused and uncomfortable, I smiled and thanked her for sharing her thoughts. Had she known I was a Muslim, she probably would've never spoken to me because I was "one of them."

Immediately afterward, I began feeling guilty. I had let my fear of confrontation prevent me from talking with her, from explaining that I was actually a Muslim and that the Jews with whom I marched were standing up for justice. I had worn my scarf in a bun when I'd felt afraid on one or two occasions before, but from then on, I decided to always wear my hijab the more common way. I wanted to overcome my fears, to let Israelis know I am a Muslim and I am not a violent person. A week later, I got that opportunity.

My internship involved traveling weekly between Jerusalem and Haifa, a two-hour bus ride on a predominantly Israeli bus route. During one of my trips, I informed a fellow passenger—who also happened to be an Israeli Defense Force (IDF) soldier—that his bag was not properly stored away, suggesting he fasten his bag before departure to avoid losing it. Arriving at our destination, we left the bus to collect our luggage. The soldier struck up a conversation with me while fiddling with his M-16. Without looking up at me, he asked where I was from and what I was doing in Israel.

"Ala'a, don't let your fears get the best of you—be confident and be yourself," I thought. My heart racing, I explained that I was an American who was in the country visiting family. He then introduced himself and said politely, "Nice to meet you" before walking away. Both the Israeli soldier and I had overcome our preconceptions to interact on a more personal, human level—all politics aside.

Muslims and Jews are so similar that sometimes we cannot tell ourselves apart. All it takes is human interaction to create understanding and appreciation of one another. I am blessed to have grown up a Muslim American within that circle of seven and to have been exposed to both Palestinian and Israeli narratives of the conflict. And I am inspired by how Islam teaches us to value people of other faiths and human life overall.

Unfortunately, we live in a world where people often judge each other. They base their opinions on misconceptions and make assumptions about one another's beliefs. Throughout my life, I have repeatedly witnessed the impact of bringing people of different backgrounds, cultures, and religions together to interact. At the age of eleven, I had befriended a diverse group of friends who empowered me with knowledge about people different from me. That experience later helped me transition to my job in Washington, DC, and even to find my place in Israel, where few Muslims feel comfortable going.

I continue to work towards a peaceful resolution to the Palestinian-Israeli conflict. I am confident I will be able to work with people who have completely opposing views because I will approach the issues not only as an Arab, a Palestinian, a Muslim, or an American, but also as a fellow human being.

Army of One
by Maryam Habib Khan

Maryam Habib Khan is a project engineer for the US Army Corps of Engineers (USACE). When she is not traveling for work, she enjoys traveling for fun with her husband, reading, caring for her toddler, and catching up on sleep. Born and raised in Maryland, Maryam has had the opportunity to travel to Pakistan every few years to visit extended family, practice her Urdu, and learn more about her heritage. She currently lives in Clarksburg, Maryland.

In 2004, I was deployed to Afghanistan on a six-month assignment with the US Army Corps of Engineers (USACE). My tour of duty came several years after the initial war was launched in response to the September 11, 2001 attacks on American soil. As my deployment neared, I experienced emotions ranging from excitement to wonder to happiness to fear.

I often questioned how I would fit into this puzzle. Would the experience be any different for me as a Muslim? Would the American soldiers be understanding about my religious practices? Would the Afghanis or Pakistanis react in a positive way? Would I fit in? Only when I returned from my first deployment did I realize the answers to all these questions were yes.

Our compound in Afghanistan was protected by former Afghan *mujahideen*, who had fought against the Soviet invasion of Afghanistan during the 1980s. About two dozen local citizens also worked and lived alongside us as engineers, interpreters, chefs, and cleaners. My initial reaction to their presence was a deep concern for our safety. I wondered repeatedly, how can we trust all of them? Wearing the DCU (Desert Camouflaged Uniform) made our identities and purpose in Afghanistan obvious. I worried we might be easy targets.

Most of the local workers did not speak English, but some did. I found ways to communicate with most of them, whether in English or my broken Dari and Urdu. Over time, I got to know them better, and my apprehension about how they would react subsided.

I learned a great deal about Afghan culture during traditional Afghan lunches and conversations with interpreters at project sites. As a Muslim, I could not always understand or agree with practices within the Afghan culture, but I was repeatedly told by the Afghanis that their country was in much better hands than it had previously been under the Taliban. Sadly, the stories and personal experiences I heard from Afghanis echoed the horrific stories about the Taliban that had been reported by the US news media.

Before my arrival, I had read about the Taliban's notorious treatment of women. Months later, I met some of these very women— women who had been forced to wear the burqa in public and who had not been allowed to work, become educated, or be treated by male doctors. I also met Afghan men who complained about the Taliban and called them hypocrites. They said the Taliban enforced strict, overbearing rules while enjoying forbidden pleasures and committing heinous acts behind closed doors.

I felt disheartened that such a rogue group could execute such terrible acts of violence and oppression. I did not feel like I shared a religion with them, for the Qur'an says, "Let there be no compulsion in religion" (2:256). By the time I arrived in Afghanistan, members of the Taliban had either gone underground or were fleeing, so the people's conditions had somewhat improved.

It was fascinating to observe the Afghanis' initial reactions to me. They regarded me with confusion, quite certain my background was Afghan or Pakistani but bewildered by my American Army uniform, flawless English, and female identity. Once they discovered and understood who I was, it was quite normal to hear comments like, "She really is a Muslim, speaks Urdu, works for the US Army, is a woman—*and* she is our boss!" All of the divergent puzzle pieces of my identity were finally fitting together in their minds. This was deeply rewarding to witness.

While many of the news headlines about the US Army presence in Iraq and Afghanistan were negative, my own everyday dealings were not. Of all the Afghanis I encountered, very few were ungrateful or unwilling to accept our help. Most were friendly, enthusiastic, and eager to learn whatever we could teach them. Afghanistan had seen an entire generation deprived of education, so it was heartwarming to see such dedication to learning.

One of my most personally fulfilling work projects was the renovation of the Rabbia-e-Balkhi Women's Hospital in Kabul. When I first frequented this hospital, it was common to find the power out or the sewage overflowing in the restrooms, spilling into the hallways and under the very beds where women were giving birth. After years without maintenance, the hospital had begun deteriorating. We refurbished the electrical, sewage, and water systems of the hospital, freeing the staff to focus on providing the best medical care possible for the women of Kabul. After completing our work, I felt a sense of accomplishment as a member of the Army Corps of Engineers, but I also felt proud to be a Muslim American woman working on a renovation project that would help my fellow sisters of Afghanistan. I knew in my heart this would truly make a difference in the everyday lives of Afghan women, their children, and their health care.

I saw up close the consideration given by US soldiers to fellow Muslim soldiers as well as to the Afghan people. At the US Army base in Kandahar, I recalled seeing signs announcing Friday prayer services for the Muslims on base. Previously closed because of missile damage, an old Afghan mosque on the Army base was being renovated and repainted by US Army soldiers—Muslims and non-Muslims alike. When we constructed Afghan National Army (ANA) brigades, we also built mosques and special ablution areas out of respect for the Afghan religion and culture. These experiences made me realize the Army was reaching out, even while it still had much to learn.

In Afghanistan, I usually covered my hair with an Army hat. It was a convenient form of head covering without having to wear both the hat and my scarf. The soldiers did not always understand why I would wear the hat indoors, since protocol required removing your cover when inside a building. Some commanders would get upset when I entered the dining halls with my hat on—they would mistake me for military personnel and think I was defying orders. They did not know I was deployed as a US Army employee—not as a soldier.

Keeping my head covered was the most difficult aspect of being a Muslim in Afghanistan, aside from trying to maintain my strict Islamic (*halal*) diet. Yet the challenges I faced gave me an opportunity to educate those same commanders about modesty in Islam. I felt I could do my part as a Muslim woman and make a positive impact on the US Army by intelligently and directly answering questions about my religion. And, in some small way, perhaps I also helped bridge gaps between the US Army and the Afghanis by representing myself as both an American and a Muslim.

My second deployment to Afghanistan between 2004 and 2006 seemed both neverending and all too short. The most unforgettable moment occurred when a former mujahideen guard approached me during Ramadan. I hadn't gotten an opportunity to get to know this older, white-haired man during my first deployment. We did not speak any languages in common, and he kept to himself. I had always assumed he did not like me.

To my surprise, he walked up to me with a big gentle smile, accompanied by another Afghan guard, who acted at his translator. He said he respected and admired the modest way I dressed, my manner of talking, my determination to stay on the halal diet, and my Muslim values, despite being born and raised in an American environment. He didn't know people like me existed, people who could balance their American and Muslim identities and not sacrifice anything while doing so.

He had waited a long time to reveal these thoughts to me. Flattered, I found myself speechless, mostly because I had not realized this guard had been watching my actions for so long and so patiently without saying a word. All of this time, I'd thought he was cold towards me, but when he finally opened his mouth, he had only positive things to say. At that moment, I felt like a walking example of a real American Muslim woman. If there was any doubt in my mind before about my ability to navigate these two identities, that brief conversation all but erased it.

I had been proud of myself for keeping up the practices of my faith, but I felt even more affirmed by the religious approval of an older Afghan man. He had reminded me that, even in the midst of this military environment, I was doing the right things—without sacrificing my standards and values.

With great certainty, I can say my identity as a Muslim, American, and Pakistani woman has been enriched by my experience in Afghanistan. Not only did I learn about a culture foreign to me, but I also experienced how these cultures responded to my own negotiated identity. I could communicate with Afghanis because of my Pakistani heritage, understand some of their religious and cultural views because of our shared faith, and provide help to the people of Afghanistan because I was an American.

2008 Campaign
by Rashida Tlaib

Rashida Tlaib was elected to the Michigan House of Representatives for the Twelfth House District (Detroit) in 2008. She was raised in Southwest Detroit, the eldest of fourteen children born to Palestinian immigrants. Rashida made history by becoming the first Muslim woman elected to the Michigan legislature. Prior to the election, she worked at a number of nonprofit organizations, including the Arab Community Center for Economic and Social Services (ACCESS) and the International Institute of Metropolitan Detroit, where she advocated to improve access to human services, education, and civil rights. In 2009, Alternatives for Girls gave Rashida the Role Model Award. She also received the National Network for Arab American Communities Emerging Leader Award, the Women of Wayne Headliner Award, and the Council on American-Islamic Relations (CAIR) Michigan Empowering Muslims Award, in addition to being named one of Crain's Detroit Business Women to Watch. Rashida received her bachelor of arts in political science from Wayne State University and her law degree from Thomas M. Cooley Law School.

The first time my boss, State Representative Steve Tobocman, asked me to run for his seat, I laughed out loud. I thought to myself, "Me? A state representative?! Ridiculous!" I didn't see how running for office could further my true goal in life, which was to start my own nonprofit. I also had a two-year-old child and a husband my demanding job already prevented me from spending enough time with.

And yet Steve's suggestion wasn't so ludicrous that I put it out of mind altogether. I weighed my decision carefully, even losing sleep over it and reciting the "dream prayer" (*salat al-istikhara*) from the Qur'an, hoping God would provide the answer in a dream.

Working for the Michigan legislature, I had seen a lot of red tape and political games hurt the very people our elected officials were supposed to be helping. I felt I needed to be working on the ground, where I could impact people's lives every day, as opposed to holding an office and watching bills sit in committees while politicians argued about whether its passage would hurt their chances at re-election. Something soon made me see things differently.

After months of working on legislation for Representative Tobocman, I saw a familiar issue hit my desk: driver's licenses for undocumented immigrants. I decided to partner with nonprofits, immigration attorneys, and the business community to reach a consensus that broadened driver's license qualifications. As the legislation passed both the House and Senate with bipartisan support, I felt fulfillment and gratification.

When one of the advocates who worked on this issue learned I had laughed at the idea of running for state representative, she said to me, "Now imagine if you hadn't been in the room when this legislation was drafted." Her words hit me hard. I suddenly realized the impact I could have on my community if I won the seat. That's when I knew, despite my resistance to the idea, that running for office was my *naseeb*, my fate. Ten days before the filing deadline, I submitted my paperwork to run for the seat of Michigan state representative for the Twelfth District (aka Southwest Detroit).

Most Detroit races are won by name recognition. Not only was my name—Rashida Tlaib (pronounced "Taleeb")—unfamiliar, but it was also difficult to pronounce. I had seven opponents, one who had already served as state representative, two who had run at least three times before, four who were African American, and three who were Hispanic. I was the odd one out—an Arab American of Muslim faith. I was running to represent an ethnically diverse community comprising 40 percent Hispanic, 30 percent African American, 30 percent white, and 2 percent Arab citizens. When word spread that I was running, I got looks that could only be interpreted as, "She is crazy if she thinks anyone is going to vote for someone like her."

My father outright said, "Baba, no one is going to vote for an Arab." My mother worried running for office meant I wasn't having another baby. I could see this was going to be an uphill battle.

I needed a game plan. I started by assembling a campaign committee of community members, friends, and family. My campaign slogan became "Southwest Detroit's Own Strength, Talent, and Diversity Working for Us." We focused on doors and dollars, with hopes that we could raise enough money to walk through the district twice or even more. I was the only candidate to start an aggressive door-to-door campaign, and I walked every street in my district twice. I hand-wrote postcards to each of the residents I met while door-knocking, handled constituent issues, made breakfast for seniors, visited churches in the district, and even gave my cell phone number to those who asked for it.

Door-knocking became the most memorable and fulfilling experience of my campaign. It was on the trail that I met an elderly man who'd just had a stroke and couldn't speak. When I returned to his home a second time, he remembered who I was and had a big smile on his face. I met working poor families living with a hole in their roof, a drug house as a neighbor, or a toxic odor from a nearby composting facility. All of them voiced a significant feeling of helplessness.

The Mauricio family really caught my attention. They had lost their son at an adult home when two staff members beat him to death. The guilt these parents felt overwhelmed all of us, and we cried together as they recounted their heartwrenching story.

With each visit and each new story I heard, I knew I had made the right decision. As a Muslim who went to law school to change the world, I realized I could start that change in the community that raised me.

Amazingly, among the blighted neighborhoods, decaying school buildings, and devastating poverty, I had developed a sense of hope. I knew that because I cared so much for my community, I would serve them wholeheartedly. It was my priority to remain accessible to my constituents. I was determined to create a fully-staffed service center, where residents could report crimes such as illegal dumping, while also receiving free tax preparation, foreclosure prevention assistance, and legal services. I fully understood the importance of "service politics" to my community. My to-do list expanded during this door-knocking phase, as did my legislative priorities.

I lost fifteen pounds walking the campaign trail, and in the process recruited some of my best volunteers: Ummsalamah, the daughter of Trinidad immigrants who had never been part of something where she could make a difference in the lives of thousands; Aramas, a Puerto Rican high school student who now wants to run for office; Lawrence, a shy African American Howard University student who recently changed his major from biology to political science; and Justin, a young Mexican American father-to-be who found inspiration to persevere through a challenging time in his life. Thinking about my volunteers always puts a smile on my face.

There were many other happy moments. When I knocked on Mr. Baksh's door, before I could say anything, he asked, "Are you Muslim?" When I said yes, he started dancing up and down.

I remember Sister Mary asking me the same thing and wondering why I didn't wear the *burqa*. I told her, "Sister Mary, it is all about interpretation." She seemed confused, and I left unsure whether she would support me. The next time I visited, she had my campaign signs up in front of her house.

During the two weeks leading to the election, I became the primary target of negative campaigns launched by my opponents. One even told my supporters that if they couldn't pronounce my name, they shouldn't vote for me. Although many of my supporters said my ethnicity didn't matter, I was still running for office in a post-9/11 era. Reporters began to call, asking if I was going to be the first Muslim elected to the Michigan legislature if my campaign was successful. I honestly didn't know, and I had no idea my victory was about to make history. I would be the first Muslim woman to serve.

Election day soon arrived, and even though we had run an impressive campaign, I was still unsure. Most candidates campaign for at least six months. I had campaigned only half that amount of time. Exhausted, I knew losing would be difficult to accept. As I walked to the campaign office storefront, I was met by a sea of "Rashida for Rep" t-shirts worn by perhaps a hundred volunteers. They were of all ages, ethnicities, and faiths. My mother was the first to approach me. She whispered in Arabic as tears streamed down her face, "I have prayed to God for you to win, and I am confident of your victory."

I delivered an emotional speech of thanks, and everyone cried with me as I said, "No matter what happens, we ran the best campaign."

After only three months of door-knocking, I won by an astonishing 44 percent of the vote. A daughter of Palestinian immigrants who didn't speak English when she started kindergarten was elected to the Michigan legislature. I am a true believer now. The American Dream exists.

As I continue to serve the community I love so dearly, I am reminded that extraordinary things *are* possible. My mother, after living in the United States for over thirty years, told me she wanted to obtain her GED. It brought tears to my eyes knowing my accomplishment had encouraged her to want more for her own life. There are many more stories out there to inspire young American Muslims—like my son, Adam, who I hope will never wait to be asked before taking on remarkable tasks that change people's lives and our world for the better.

Dual Identities
by Reem Odeh

*Reem Odeh is a lawyer and an advocate for the Arab American
community. As one of six children, she was born in Fairfax, Virginia, to Palestinian immigrants. She received her bachelor's degree in psychology and mass communications from Saint Xavier
University and her juris doctorate from The John Marshall Law
School. Reem speaks and writes Arabic fluently and is a member
of the Arab-American, Illinois State, American, and Chicago Bar
Associations. She has worked with Amnesty International and remains active in human rights causes and organizations, including
the Arab American Democratic Club and the Palestinian America
Women's Association. In 2008, Reem was nominated as a delegate
to the Democratic National Convention. A proud Chicago mom,
she loves traveling with her three supportive, patient, and understanding children.*

I n my family, it was my maternal great-grandfather who first
took the journey from Palestine to America. After arriving at
Ellis Island in New York, he continued on to Maryland. I was
born in America, and many years after my great-grandfather

came to this country, I would make the reverse journey, traveling from America back to Palestine to visit my ancestors' homeland for the first time.

I was four the summer we flew Air France to my grandparents' village home in al-Bireh. I cried nonstop from America to the Middle East, greatly distressing the two elderly relatives who had been entrusted with my care. I was sad because I had never been away from my parents, and I was scared by the prospect of going to a strange and unfamiliar land.

My first ride from the airport to the village was unforgettable. We passed beautiful mountains and trees, juxtaposed against truckfuls of Israeli Army soldiers pointing machine guns at us. I had never experienced driving through checkpoints or being stopped randomly by soldiers who inspected our vehicles and bags. By the time I had acclimated to this new land and its people, we were preparing to board the return flight home.

I never realized how different I was from my American peers until I returned from al-Bireh and started kindergarten. I was in elementary and secondary school when the gaps between my Islamic teachings and my American cultural leanings became more apparent. Despite succeeding academically and even skipping a grade, I felt uncertain about my place at school and in the larger society. These feelings both concerned and confused me.

I felt like a child being forced to pick between two divorced parents. Growing up as a Muslim girl in America forced me to choose between two lifestyles and identities that both seemed natural to me. While I was taught in Islamic school that I could practice my faith anywhere, the American culture surrounding me gave me the impression that my religion didn't have a place in it.

Many aspects of my home life did not reconcile with the cultural norms practiced by my classmates. For instance, I was forbidden from attending a birthday party at another girl's home because of fears that she may have male family members who would pose a threat to me. Mixing with the opposite sex was culturally unacceptable to my parents, so co-ed events like high school football games, homecoming dances, long overnight trips, and parties were off-limits—and dating was out of the question.

Despite not participating in some aspects of American culture, I experienced unexpected opportunities because of my Muslim Arab identity. Kids in my classes asked me questions about Islam, and in return, I asked them questions about Christianity and Hinduism. In this way, we learned from one another, and I helped counteract many of their cultural prejudices.

When we studied the Israeli-Palestinian conflict in my high school Social Studies class, I realized many of my fellow Americans perceive the conflict as extremist groups disrupting the peace of a democratic rival. I was strongly compelled to share the Palestinian perspective with my classmates, and I summoned my childhood experiences in the West Bank to paint a picture of what life is like for the Palestinians there. I talked about attending Friday prayers at the Dome of the Rock and traveling to Bethlehem to visit the Church of the Nativity. I described my extended family in al-Bireh, whose hospitality and love continues to envelop me, even as we are thousands of miles apart.

My father often said he did not want his children to be like "those Americans who don't even know where they're from." I know he is grateful that my frequent trips to Palestine have helped me retain my culture. Yet I also know he would prefer that I hadn't seen firsthand many of the hardships our family has endured.

Although I was taught to look beyond the war-torn society, my trips exposed me to the painful realities of war, realities my textbooks seldom mentioned. Seared into my mind is the image of a Palestinian boy with an Uzi pointed at his head by an Israeli soldier. Yet the peace and tranquility of my parents' village taught me that war was only one aspect of Palestinian life. Those childhood visits to al-Bireh humanized the subjects of my Social Studies class, giving me a deeper understanding of Muslims outside the US.

During my visits to al-Bireh, I came to realize the Muslim world painted America as a country that was free and beautiful but lacked morals, while many of my fellow Americans perceived Islam as an antiquated, backwards religion full of conservatives and extremists. My firsthand knowledge and unique background enabled me to show my classmates a different side of the story.

At thirteen, I was just starting to see myself as a whole person, just beginning to make sense of the culture and society in which I existed. Like my education, my life began skipping ahead, too. My identity split back into dualities as I experienced an entirely new form of societal isolation. Soon after my fourteenth birthday, I got married.

A suitor who wanted to marry me had approached my parents. I agreed to the marriage because I believed that was how it was supposed to be done. The marriage was meant to protect my honor, which was highly prized in my father's household.

I was a married fourteen-year-old high school student, and despite my intellectual maturity, it was obvious I had skipped more than just a grade this time. While I was convinced I was doing was the right thing, I felt a constant disconnect between my body and my mind. Being a cheerleader, attending homecoming dances, listening to rock music, and reading *Young Miss* magazine seemed like natural choices at that age.

Again, I felt the tug of dual identities, this time between my role as a wife and my life as a teenager. I felt my marriage had cut off the flow of blood to half of my heart. I wanted to be enjoying my teenage years like my classmates, but I did not want to disappoint my parents. Yes, I had willingly agreed to the marriage, as had my husband, but neither of us knew what we were doing. Two years later, while other girls were planning their sweet sixteen parties, I was tending to my newborn son. Soon after his birth, my identity changed again: I became a divorced teenage mom.

As a single mother in the Muslim community, I began to realize my burdens. My divorce left me stigmatized and isolated within my own culture. It was during these years that my inner turmoil was the greatest. The community scorned me, and ultimately, my highly cherished honor had not been protected. I began to believe the modern Muslim male was infatuated with purity and virginity. Others viewed me as a lost soul and "used goods."

Eventually, I married a new man in a traditional Muslim wedding celebration. That sealed my position as a second-class citizen. My husband expected me to be obligated to him for taking me in, which he took as permission to do whatever he pleased. He abused and treated me as though my existence did not matter in this world. Not surprisingly, my self-esteem plummeted.

Although traumatizing, this second marriage gave me an opportunity to grow as a woman. I had allowed Old World customs to harm my well-being. Yet I knew Islam taught that women should be treated better.

I remembered my parents' loving relationship. My father is a hard-working husband and father, and he never once abused my strong and independent mother. I had grown up during a time that saw women taking advantage of the previous generation's liberation movement. My American upbringing had taught me that education would empower women to gain equality with men.

I am thankful for my family's support as I struggled through a second divorce and, later, law school. My Islamic side guided me through the rough times, and my American side gave me power I never imagined during my early teenage years. As I have grown up, these two identities have solidly fused together, and I'm no longer choosing sides, no longer feeling isolated.

The sense of duality is still present in me, but as a practicing lawyer, I now fight for the rights of Muslims across the US, fueled by the confidence gained through my American education. My inner turmoil is diminishing, and I can envision a future where I feel fully secure in being precisely who I am: an American Muslim, whose roots extend across the globe to a Palestinian village called al-Bireh.

Creating Sarah
by Sarah Kajani

Sarah Kajani received a bachelor's degree in international relations and a minor in English from Mount Holyoke College. Born near Pittsburgh, Pennsylvania, and raised near Atlanta, Georgia, she is a proud nerd, creative thinker, coffee addict, and avid reader. Sarah is currently pursuing a career in marketing and public relations.

"Life is not about finding yourself. Life is about creating yourself." This quote represents the struggle of my life. I grew up as a child of two names, one who went by the name Sarah, pronounced SAY-rah, and the other who went by the name Sara, pronounced SAW-rah. I was two personalities in one small body.

Sarah was a name with Islamic roots, but it was easy for Americans to pronounce. My parents chose that name, its spelling, and the traditional Western pronunciation as a nod to the country they had immigrated to many years earlier. It was also part of their quest for acceptance in a culture they little understood.

Sara, on the other hand, was my Muslim name, its Indian pronunciation representing my Islamic life. It was also given to me by my parents in hopes of salvaging a culture from the country they had left behind. Along with Sara came my Indian culture and my parents' Ismaili Islam faith.

I knew early on it wasn't going to be easy growing up as a hyphenated persona: an Indian-Ismaili-Muslim-American in the US. I remember the first time I wore henna to the private school I attended. I was in the first grade. My mom trailed uncharacteristically behind, escorting me to class so she could explain to my teacher what I had on my hands. She'd hoped the teacher could keep the children from teasing me.

I did not share my mother's concerns. I wore the henna proudly and answered many curious questions about it. Questions like, "Is that poop?", "Why do you have brown stuff all over your hand?", and "Eww, I can't sit next to you. You're all weird."

One of my favorite traditions, henna tattooing was tied to every religious holiday my family celebrated. During the day of application, all of my female relatives would sit together, laughing and talking as we painted beautiful henna designs on our hands. These were the memories I wanted to share with my classmates when I wore the henna to school that day. As people started asking questions, I began realizing my hand art wasn't normal to them. Surprisingly, I actually liked the attention—and the power it gave me to chase away the boys who found it icky. As a first-grader, I didn't fully understand why people didn't think my hands were cool, but I soon realized it made me appear even more different than I, the only minority in my class, already was.

Although my school and Ismaili environments were two very different spheres of socialization, they were equally cliquish. As I grew older, I felt a need to be accepted at both, which meant not being seen as the minority "freak" at school. I wanted to hang out with the cool kids. I fed off of acceptance, whether that came from bribing people with gifts or feigning agreement with the popular kids.

My naive desire for acceptance came to a head in the fifth grade, when I began attending public school. I had finally succumbed to peer pressure, relinquishing my own self-confidence. Other people's opinions were all that mattered to me, so I suppressed my own. I pretended I had been born in India because my classmates found that exotic. I gained entry into the popular cliques at school. My twelve-year-old brain never calculated that it was my confidence and personality that really mattered. In my obsession to be accepted, I ended up becoming an outsider. I never created my own identity; instead, I allowed myself to be defined by others' whims.

My Muslim life mirrored this experience. At jamatkhana, I remained an outsider. I never got along with the girls my age. Hanging out with boys wasn't an option culturally, so I was stuck feeling alone and rejected. Even though most of the girls were American-born, too, they didn't try to forge a balance between the two worlds as I had. Instead, they just picked one: the South Asian Muslim identity. Most of the girls didn't understand how I could have both American and Muslim friends. I remember my awkward fourth-grade attempt to invite both groups of friends to a party one time. My American friends were open to learning more about my other life, but my Muslim friends didn't want anything to do with my non-Muslim classmates.

Still struggling to find a place for myself, I began to make older friends, but this attempt was short-lived. I was constantly pushed by my mother to befriend girls my own age. Desperate, I would do anything these girls asked, whether that meant giving up prized possessions, sneaking outside our prayer hall during prayer, or being "it" every time we played a game of tag. Ultimately, I never found acceptance in either realm because my two different lives kept colliding.

This clash became evident in high school when I wanted to join the track team. I remember telling my mom that the meets were held on Fridays or Saturdays, hoping she would agree since I wouldn't be missing many classes each week.

"I am sorry. You can't do it," my mom said. "Those days are for prayer only." Nothing, even my feeble attempts at revolt, could change her mind. As Sarah, a teenager in high school, I started disliking how Islam interfered with my school life. I resented how my religious life always took precedence over everything else. If I'd wanted to participate in a jamatkhana-initiated sports tournament, my parents would've easily said yes. Sara was turning into my enemy—it was as if her world always stopped Sarah's life from progressing.

As Sara, my life wasn't any easier. My ignorance of popular Indian culture posed a different obstacle to acceptance. I remember my jamatkhana friends discussing the latest Bollywood song and movie.

"Have you seen it or heard about it?" one of the girls asked me.

"Nope."

"Ha! Of course not. You are such an ABCD[1]." I laughed off the insult, but I was hurt deeply. They judged me as less Indian because I did not have satellite Indian channels or had not learned the native languages.

My father didn't believe in teaching me Hindi, Urdu, or Gujarati. He believed English was the only language I should know because that was the language that would take me the farthest. Neither of us predicted how interdependent the world would become and how important being bilingual and even trilingual would later become. As a child, I loved eavesdropping on my parents, but they were usually speaking in Hindi or Gujarati. I secretly began to teach myself these languages. I was too embarrassed to

[1] The slang term "ABCD" stands for "American Born Confused Desi." It is an insult used to describe US-born individuals of South Asian descent who are perceived to be acting "too American."

practice in front of my friends, though. Instead of Bollywood songs, I sang hip-hop lyrics. My jamatkhana friends began to accept me as the one who kept them updated on American social life. Sarah's world was beginning to coalesce with Sara's.

At school, I acted like I understood my friends' conversations about 1970s and 1980s music and culture, but I was actually clueless. I may have been born in America, but I was raised in old-fashioned Indian culture. I never fully absorbed some of America's culture. When it became obvious that I didn't know certain things about American cultural history, I began talking about Bollywood and its culture, music, and acting as if I were an expert. At school, I became known as the girl who knew everything about Indian culture and a little about the American way of life.

Despite learning different languages and trying to absorb everything about both Indian and American culture, I never felt wholly accepted anywhere. People still acted surprised when I knew something about either culture. Even as a college student, my friends would hear me singing along to a Bollywood track and scream, "Oh my God! You know this song? Since when? You have finally become well-rounded."

I didn't speak enough Arabic or know enough about Indian movies for Sara's life, nor did I know enough about American culture for Sarah's life. Balance was the essential message of my religion, but I had never figured out how to reach a balance between my two identities.

Finally, in high school, a shift began to take place. Confidence and self-acceptance began to form once I realized I can never change my core self. I am who I am. Being Muslim makes me unique in American culture—it gives me a sense of peace and makes me feel I always have a place where I belong. Being American makes me unique in my family—it gives me a new culture and fresh traditions. I needed to realize it was okay to be different. I needed to understand that my two identities could coexist without conflict.

As a senior at high school—three years after 9/11—I began to develop more pride in myself as a Muslim. On my college applications, I confidently ticked the Islam box under the religion section, despite my mother's protests. "Raja beta, don't check this box because the college won't accept you."

"Mom, why does it really matter? 9/11 was three years ago. I am who I am, Ma."

Now that I'm older, I realize acceptance is insignificant. What really matters is happiness and confidence. I should be able to stand up and proudly state who I am, what I am, and what religion and culture I ascribe to—without hesitation. I may never be able to reach a perfect balance between my marginalized identities, but I'm not sure I want to. If my life had been balanced all along, I would not be able to appreciate both of those identities as much as I do now. Struggling to maintain my duality has shaped me into who I am today. This balance of identities *is* my identity. I can accept who I am and define myself by my own standards. I can step out into the world as both Sarah and Sara while being completely satisfied with who I am. Who cares if I'm not good enough for other people, as long as I am good enough for myself?

I now address myself as "Saw-rah," spelled "Sarah." That doesn't mean one identity has prevailed over the other. Rather, it is a merging of the two names that represents me as a whole. Sarah, pronounced "Say-rah," was my exterior self, what I was to the world: an Indian-*American*. Sara, pronounced "Saw-rah," was my interior self and what dictated my moral and religious life. I loved both identities equally, and each spoke to a different part of me. Joined together, they represent a girl who loves every last bit of herself, a girl who doesn't care what others think, a girl who has finally created her self.

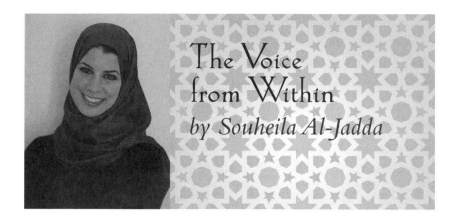

The Voice
from Within
by Souheila Al-Jadda

Souheila Al-Jadda is a journalist and award-winning television producer. Her opinion columns have been published in newspapers worldwide including USA Today, The Christian Science Monitor, *and* The Dallas Morning News, *among others. Souheila is also a Senior Editor of* The Islamic Monthly Magazine. *She is a member of the Board of Contributors for* USA Today. *Souheila serves on the Board of Directors of* Illume Magazine, *an award-winning, independent magazine that captures and articulates the Muslim-American experience. She is also a producer with Link TV, earning a George F. Peabody award for the program,* Mosaic, World News from the Middle East. *She also produced the* Who Speaks for Islam? *series for the station. Souheila is a global expert for the United Nations Alliance of Civilizations and has appeared as a guest analyst on various national radio and television networks on topics relating to women, Islam, and the Middle East. In 2008, she was selected as a global Muslim Leader of Tomorrow. She earned a bachelor's in Journalism and Political Science from the George Washington University and a master's in International Relations and Economics from the Johns Hopkins University School of Advanced International Studies.*

I began my journalism career in fifth grade. My hometown newspaper in Ohio, the *Norwalk Reflector*, was holding a writing contest, which I entered by writing an editorial about then-President Ferdinand Marcos of the Philippines. I won the contest and published my first op-ed piece at the age of eleven. Two years later, my best friend and I were starting a newspaper at the Catholic school we attended. It was an immediate hit with our classmates but a complete bust with the teachers.

The school administration forced us to shut down our makeshift newspaper almost as soon as it had begun. This short-lived venture taught me a lesson about the importance of making yourself heard at a time when authority figures do not seem to want to listen.

My writing style and approach to journalism has certainly improved since my younger days, but my relentless desire to ask questions and be heard remains. Today, I take out my journalist's notebook after having experienced traumatic cultural shocks like the tragic events of September 11. That also marks the day when I began feeling like a stranger in the country I had always called home.

"Are you a terrorist?"

"Are you going to blow this bus up?"

"Do you have a bomb in your bag?"

A group of giggling teenagers bombarded me with questions as I rode a public bus to work. I sat silently, staring straight ahead, pretending their remarks did not hurt me. Although my veil may have set me apart, I knew it was my faith that was the object of their ridicule. With nearly seven million other Muslim Americans being subjected to similar stereotypes, I also knew I was not alone. During the ten-minute bus ride, I found strength by remembering Rosa Parks, the black woman who shocked 1955 America by taking her rightful place at the front of a public bus.

These teenagers' taunts did not come out of nowhere. They partly resulted from repeated exposure to distorted representations of Islam and Muslims. At the time, the US government and media cast a shadow of fear and suspicion over American Muslims and Arabs. Some public officials portrayed the global war on terror as a religious crusade against Islam. Newspaper headlines like "All-American Osamas"[1] and book titles like *American Jihad*[2] screamed xenophobia.

This paranoid atmosphere led to an immediate backlash against Muslims and Arabs in the US. Many Muslims felt compelled to mask their Islamic identity. Women removed their hijabs and men shaved off their beards. I, too, began questioning my own identity and place in this country. Who was I? An American first? A Muslim? An Arab? My hijab and my religion were a source of fear for people. Should I consider taking my headscarf off, even for a short period?

At the age of twenty-six, I had chosen to wear hijab, making a lifelong commitment to my faith and myself. To break that commitment would mean those teens on the bus would have succeeded in weakening my faith. I would not allow that to happen.

Being an American of Arab descent, I have often felt caught between two worlds, struggling to blend into the American melting pot while also maintaining my Arab and Islamic identities. At times, I want to be seen as all-American, minimizing my ethnic background. It's pretty easy until someone asks my name. I reluctantly recite my "How-to-Pronounce-Souheila" monologue: "SUE as in Suzanne, HAY as in hay for horses, and LA as in la-la-la-la." The next question people ask is where I am from. I usually say, "I was born in Ohio" and quickly switch the subject.

---

[1] Nicholas D. Kristof, "All-American Osamas." In the *New York Times*. June 7, 2002.

[2] Steven Emerson. *American Jihad: The Terrorists Living Among Us* (New York: *The Free Press*, 2002).

All of this changed after I started wearing hijab. Now, most people assume I am a foreigner. They ask where I am from without even bothering to ask my name. This frustrates me, especially since America is a land of immigrants and their children, like me, who have been born and raised in this country. I feel just as American as anyone else.

Visiting relatives in the Middle East, I always find myself trying to gain acceptance in my parents' Arab culture. First, there is the language barrier. With my pronunciation lacking the lightness of a native tongue, it often draws giggles from my Arab cousins. Also, being an American carries a stigma in the Middle East. I often bear the brunt of criticism of America's foreign policy and its cultural and moral failings. In defense of the US, I always try to distinguish the American people from the policies of the American government. That's when I am reminded that the American people elect their government, freely and fairly, unlike the people in many Arab countries.

I have dealt with these challenges for many years while seeking answers to questions about my identity. As a student at a Catholic elementary school for eight years, I understood I was different from my classmates. I had many questions about my faith. Why couldn't I genuflect in church? Why couldn't I eat the body and bread of Christ? Or the blood and wine of Christ, for that matter? I was always the odd one out—sitting in the pew while the rest of my classmates took the Eucharist or not being allowed to perform in the Christmas plays. These rituals made Christianity appealing. At the time, I felt Islam lacked the fun Christianity offered.

My family could be considered Ramadan Muslims, only practicing our religion during the holy month of Ramadan, when we would fast from sunrise until sunset. My parents often reminded me that Islam and Christianity were practically the same religion, except for that minor detail about Muslims not believing the prophet Jesus died on the cross or that he was the son of God. While my classmates were going through the rites of confirmation, my mother visited my school to deliver a talk about Islam to my class. I sometimes wonder whether she did this more to reinforce my Islamic identity than to educate others about my religion.

In school, I followed the old adage, "Do as the Romans do." Or rather, "Do as the Norwalkians do." And I did for many years. Nonetheless, attending church every week and taking religion classes did not make me feel any closer to the Christian faith. I felt more like an outsider looking in.

I spent my summers in the Middle East, where I would watch my older aunts and uncles praying on their carpets, facing Mecca. For several minutes, they would stand, bow, and prostrate themselves on the ground whispering Arabic prayers beneath their breath. They always looked somber and somewhat sad—a stark contrast to the celebratory nativity plays and hymns I had grown accustomed to at church services.

Ironically, I still felt like a distant outsider looking in on a faith that should have been familiar to me. I wanted to learn more but was always too embarrassed to ask. In the Arab world, it is often assumed everyone knows about religion and prayers at a very young age, be they Christian or Muslim.

For me, however, real understanding about Islam did not arrive until college, when I came face to face with other American Muslims like myself. I began re-examining myself and my identity. As I befriended more Muslims, my desire to learn and understand more about my own religion increased. I took classes in Islam and Arabic, the language of the Qur'an. I became an active member of my university's Muslim Students Association. I grew stronger in faith and closer to God. For once, I felt a connection to my religion I had never experienced before. It took finding a sense of community to ignite a spiritual connection to my religion.

Having enrolled at a university in the nation's capital—where politics and protests are an everyday affair—I was constantly reminded about the lesson I took away when my newspaper was shut down in elementary school: everyone has a right to speak and be heard.

After many years of self-examination, I have come to realize I do not have to limit my identity to being wholly American, Arab, or Muslim. Like most children of immigrants, I am a mosaic of many different identities, pieced together with the glue of life experiences, family, history, community, and love.

After 9/11, I decided not to hide but to stand up and stand out by expressing a voice rarely heard in American newspapers or television newscasts. I began writing my own thoughts down and offering them as an honest perspective on my own experiences, religion, and culture. To me, writing was not just a form of expression, but it was also a therapeutic way to vent my concerns about what was happening in our country.

Perhaps my articles will help foster a wider dialogue about what is taking place in our country and abroad. Perhaps someone will read an article and learn something new. If that happens, I will have accomplished my goal as a journalist.

Congressman Keith Ellison of Minnesota, America's first Muslim representative, once said that as Muslims in America, we all have stories to tell. "If we are not writing, if we are not talking, if we are not telling our story, then no one will hear it," he said. "The Muslim story in America is a story of a people continuing to fight for justice, to fight for equal opportunity, to fight for world peace.... We have to tell it."

Representative Ellison was reiterating an important principle expressed in Islam's sacred text: "O mankind! We created you from a single [pair] of a male and a female, and made you into nations and tribes, that ye may know each other (not that ye may despise [each other])" (Qur'an 49:13).

I have attempted to put these divine words into action by learning more about the world and letting others know more about me. Perhaps my words, in a small way, will contribute to a larger dialogue that can help fill the gap of understanding between my own ethnic and religious communities and the wider American public.

One article at a time, I will continue to tell my story. I encourage you to tell yours.

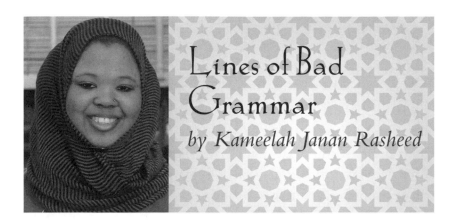

Lines of Bad Grammar

by Kameelah Janan Rasheed

Kameelah Janan Rasheed was born in East Palo Alto, California. She lived in Cape Town, South Africa, as an exchange student; in Johannesburg, South Africa, as an Amy Biehl US Fulbright Scholar; and in Washington, DC, as a Harry S. Truman Scholar. After teaching for three years in California, she relocated to Brooklyn, New York, to accept a new teaching position. Kameelah earned her bachelor of arts in public policy–Africana studies from Pomona College, and she holds an EdM in secondary education from Stanford University. Her documentary photography has been exhibited in California, New York, and Washington, DC, and published in F-Stop *and* make/shift *magazines as well as in Zimbabwean and South African publications. Kameelah is a cofounder of Mambu Badu, a photography collective for emerging female photographers of African descent. She also serves as the visual arts editor for Aaduna, a journal for emerging writers and artists. Her published writings can be found in* The Nation *(online),* Pambazuka: Pan-African Voices for Freedom and Justice *(www.pambazuka. org),* WireTap, Illume, *and* make/shift. *Kameelah can be found online at* kameelahr.com/home.html.

In 1998, I began Catholic high school as one of four "low-income" black students. I was the only Muslim, an indie rock lover, and founder of the Muslim-Jewish Alliance. By my sophomore year of college, I was a feminist and Pan-African nationalist who worked at the Women's Center, drank copious amounts of tea, and listened to Fiona Apple. As a Fulbright scholar in South Africa, I stumbled onto Marxism, befriended a hip-hop group in Soweto, chatted with Rastafarians about syncretism, and developed an interest in baptismal ceremonies.

By graduate school, I was just an angst-ridden amorphous mess that had atomized into bits. I was crumbling under the pressure of explaining the logic of my existence. My identities were clumsily colliding in this obnoxiously choreographed dance. Yet they seemed to work well together—like the occasional plaid and tweed combination. It was others who made the combination seem blasphemous. This situation ushered in an opportunity to ask the kinds of existential questions that make for quirky independent films. With pratfalls more common than graceful pirouettes, I journeyed towards reconciliation.

During this journey, I fell in love with e.e. cummings's syntactic innovations, experimental punctuation, and defiance of lineation and margins. Emily Dickinson's unusual juxtapositions, manipulation of word classes, and abrupt line breaks were strangely seductive. Harryette Mullen delicately emptied words of their popular meaning, only to refill them with punchy textual concoctions. There was something magical and mildly mischievous about what they were doing as writers. Part of me wondered whether what they did with words was what I was hoping to achieve in the negotiation of my identity—bypassing conventional grammar logic in lieu of something more elastic, more elegant, and dare I say, more truthful.

The grammar of identity is about the punctuation—the periods, colons, hyphens, and commas—that create undesirable borderlands between identities. My blackness too readily trespasses into the sovereign nation of Islam, carelessly invades the principalities of femininity, and preemptively attacks the unclaimed territories of my identity. I endured airport security checks, racial authenticity authorization, and religious piety interrogations. I migrated to the margins, stumbled over commas, hid in the confines of parentheses, found temporary refuge in the footnotes no one bothers to read, and hung wishful thoughts on the stubborn quotation marks to which my ungainly words are beholden. We speak of erasure through footnoting and exile. We institutionalize style guides and identity documents.

There is a proper way of existing: in a perfectly constructed sentence with carefully placed punctuation and immaculate grammar. Blackness has a home, and Islam has a home. Neither shall trespass sentence boundaries nor mingle, even with the aid of a comma. Gender expression is completely muted. Security in national identity shifts as abruptly as orange terror alerts.

In an obsessive-compulsive world driven by binaries and multiple-choice approaches to identity, I was told to choose one:

  (a) I am Muslim.
  (b) I am black.
  (c) I am American.
  (d) I am a woman.
  (e) I am none of the above.

Much like my moments of hesitation on the SAT, I failed to choose any, convinced this was an illusory sense of choice to begin with.

As a black Muslim woman in America, I am a run-on sentence that others constantly try to edit. Self-proclaimed editors take their pens to me as they would to a manuscript: erasing and marking. For a while, I readily offered up myself for editing because I'd internalized the grammar of identity, believing linearity was more important than truth. I footnoted elements of my Muslim identity to feel more accepted among black folks. I arrested elements of my blackness inside the shield of parentheses to appease non-black Muslims, all while speaking softly so as not to scare white children at airports while I am being held in a plexiglass cell for my "headgear" check. My self-editing was only reified by the external editing. I did not hate myself; rather, I hated that my self had been edited out of the public discourse.

No one told me how to be in this *dunya*. Much was learned by trial and error. I discovered that if my scarf was not wrapped in a particular away, I risked being ignored when I entered a mosque with a non-black majority. I came to realize many Muslims assumed I am not a "real" Muslim because my parents are converts to Islam. My father taught me to read Arabic, but I did not publicly recite because I feared someone would criticize my recitation of the Qur'an in Arabic, my *tajweed*. Speaking up about Muslim-owned liquor stores or the categorization of urban poverty issues as "not on the Muslim agenda" often alienated me. While I wore my hijab neatly pinned under my chin as many Arab and South Asian women do, I still caught askew glances because I wore jeans and a clever thrift store t-shirt instead of an abaya. I felt uncomfortable living in a community where part of me had to be silenced.

There was an entire year when I did not go to the masjid at all. I felt myself growing increasingly frustrated and wanted to take the time to differentiate between Islam and Muslims. Islam is the perfect religion. The behavior of Muslims needn't be confused with the faith itself. Many times, they do not align. During that year, I grew the most in my spirituality—improving my concentration during prayer (*khushoo*), reflecting on my role in this world, and exploring intersections with other faiths. I also felt a sense of clarity and was inspired to write my first sermon (*khutbah*), which examined our unhealthy attachment to dunya. During this journey, a friend suggested I read Sufi aphorisms from Ibn Ata'llah. One passage particularly resonated with me: "when He alienates you from his creatures, then know that He wants to open for you the door to intimacy with Him." I'd spent so much time trying to build relationships with other Muslims, many of whom had rejected me, that I hadn't spent time nurturing my relationship with God.

Outside the Muslim community, some were convinced I had bartered my authentic blackness for "Arab voodoo." They prayed for my whitened soul, proposed induction into Rastafarianism as my salvation, and argued that penetration could correct my treasonous behavior. In the event that the Arab voodoo completely infiltrated my vulnerable soul and the sexual exorcism failed, I could no longer be helped. I would become a lost cause.

Growing up, I chatted about books while cleaning pipettes in the science lab, read Carolina Biological Supply Company catalogs, graduated from middle school at twelve, and spent my clothing allowance on school supplies. Uninterested in seeking approval, I sought refuge in Paul Beatty's "designated neighborhood safe houses on the ghetto geeks' underground railroad."

The beautiful thing about disrupting the grammar of what is deemed authentic Islam or blackness is you are exiled. In exile, I was beholden to no one but God. My mistake all along had been assuming otherwise. Around twenty-three, I slowly reflected that there was something sickeningly theatrical about the way I had to repackage myself for different audiences. It was time-consuming and dishonest to travel between public and private selves.

When I was younger, I decided I was depressed. (It was the self-help revolution of the nineties, and I read a lot.) In reality, it wasn't depression; rather, it was nostalgia for the days of being eight years old and living without the fear of being myself— wearing shorts in the rain, playing in mud puddles, and begging my dad to drive all the way back home so I could wear my hijab at mosque for Friday's congregational prayer service (*jumu'ah*). I yearned for the Kameelah who only existed around a few close friends and in unpublished writings.

I imagined that if e.e. cummings or Emily Dickinson were to write a poem that personified my public identity, they'd be bored, as there were no opportunities for flippant defiance of lineation, no spaces for unusual juxtapositions, and certainly no entry points for a beautifully crafted run-on sentence. I know my identity possesses lines of bad grammar—confusing syntax, uncanny collocation.

In private, I was a delightful run-on sentence uninterrupted by proper grammar: I listened to Nasheeds and Sufjan Stevens, wore Chuck Taylors with dresses, explored gendered Qur'anic exegeses, had close male friends, was slightly taken aback by separate entrances at masjids, chose veganism, didn't believe marriage had to happen by twenty or that a wife had to stay at home, found the struggle in Darfur to be of equal importance to the struggle in Palestine, maintained strong relationships with LGBT friends, attended indie rock concerts, took snail walks, practiced photography, dreamed of traveling the world solo, taught high school kids, and loved dogs. I wasn't an undercover "progressive Muslim" or a feminist; those titles irk me. Simply, I was someone who asked a lot of questions. My parents had taught me well, as had the Qur'an. That me existed alongside—not in opposition to—Ramadan fasting, five daily prayers, devotional chanting (*dhikr*), and black hijabs.

The private me is now public. As Mullen writes in her poem, "My Body Reads Like a Poem": "My skin has lines of bad grammar, / but he recites it with a straight face. / He is serious and uses no rhyme." I only ask that my lines of bad grammar be read with sincerity.

Glossary

abaya. Refers to any long, loose-fitting coat or garment worn by some Muslim women. It covers the whole body except the face, feet and hands. These terms can be used interchangeably, depending on the region or culture in which they are used. Jilbab has the same meaning.

'abd. Literally, slave or servant. In Islam, everything is seen as far from the essence and power of God. Humans are nothing when compared to the All-Powerful One God; all are slaves, servants, before God. The term *'abd* is often paired with *khalifa* (leader, vicegerent or representative of God). The idea is that humans can become *khalifa* but only through knowing and loving God and others in a state of humble servitude.

adhan. The call to prayer chanted from the minaret of mosques.

Aga Khan. The spiritual leader of Nizari Shi'ism.

Alhamdulillah. "Praise be to God." A term often used by Muslims to express thanks to God.

Allah. The Arabic word for God. In the Qur'an, Allah is understood as the God of Abraham, Moses and Jesus and all true prophets.

ameen. A declaration of affirmation, similar to the word "Amen" found in the Bible.

burqa. A dress which covers the whole face and body.

chador. Mainly used in Iran (chador is a Persian term for garment or cloak). A chador is a full-length semi-circle of fabric open down the front, which is thrown over the head and held closed in front.

deen. Faith or religion.

dhikr. Devotional chanting of short phrases or sacred words from the Qur'an.

dupata. Hindi and Urdu term for long scarf.

fajr. Dawn, a reference to the first of the five prayers of the day.

hadith. Sayings and acts of the Prophet Muhammad and his companions collected after his death that serve as guidance for understanding the Qur'an and Islamic law.

hajj. The pilgrimage to Islam's birthplace, the holy city of Mecca. This spiritual journey is the fifth pillar of Islam, a requirement of every Muslim to perform, if within their means, at least once in their lifetime.

halal. Refers to Islamic dietary laws or, more specifically, meat that has been slaughtered in a prescribed way. Can also refer to anything proper or legitimate and according to Islamic law.

halaqa. A study group with the primary purpose of learning about Islam.

iftaar. The evening meal to break the fast during Ramadan

jannah. Literally, "garden" in Arabic. The Islamic conception of Jannah is paradise—or heaven.

jihad. The Arabic term for "struggle in the path of God." The Qur'an speaks of the greater and lesser jihads. The greater jihad is the personal struggle to overcome one's own imperfections and shortcomings, the effort by Muslims to perfect their submission (islam) and their faith (iman). The lesser jihad is the battle against the enemies of Islam as regulated by the shariah, as in defensive war.

jilbab. See abaya.

jumu'ah. Friday congregational prayer held just after noon

khushoo. Concentration in prayer.

khutbha. The sermon given at mosque on Friday.

ma'atam. The rhythmic beating of the chest done mostly by Shi'is and Sufis to recall the sufferings of the family of the Prophet.

masha' Allah. An Islamic expression of appreciation for a person or a circumstance, meaning "God has willed it."
masjid. Also referred to as a mosque, a place of prayer and worship.

muslimah. A female believer.

namahram. Persian term for someone who is not a blood relative.

namaz. Persian term for prayer.

naseeb. Fate or destiny.

niqab. The veil that covers the face of a woman.

rakat sunnah. Portions of prayer that are not obligatory but beneficial to do.

Ramadan. The month of fasting for Muslims.

salat. The five daily prayers said by Muslims.

shahada. The first pillar of Islam, the act of declaring one's faith, which consists of two statements: "There is no god but God" (*la ilaha illa'llah*) followed by "and Muhammad is the Prophet of God (*Muhammadun rasul Allah*).

sheikh. An elder or scholar.

Shi'a. The Shi'a are Muslims who follow the line of succession after Muhammad's death through his son-in-law and cousin Ali ibn Abi Talib.

suhur. The early morning meal during Ramadan.

sunnah. The body of Islamic custom and practice based on Muhammad's words and deeds as recorded in the Qur'an and hadith collections.

Sunni. The Sunnis are Muslims who follow the line of succession after Muhammad's death through the process of consensus of the companions of Muhammad. The first Sunni caliph was Abu Bakr, a close companion and father-in-law of the Prophet.

tajweed. The art of proper pronunciation of Arabic recitation of the Qur'an.

ummah. The Muslim community.

ziyarat. Pilgrimage to sites associated with Muhammad, his family and companions and saints.

Questions for Discussion

1. What is religion? What is the purpose of religion? What is the difference between religious doctrine and what people of faith do in practice?

2. What is culture? How is it intertwined with religion? Is it so intertwined in the United States? How do the women in *I Speak for Myself* address the act of balancing their faith with their American identity?

3. What was your perception of Islam before reading *I Speak for Myself* and has it been changed or confirmed after reading the book? In what ways, if any, has it changed?

4. What information or argument or perspective in the book did you find especially surprising or compelling? And furthermore, with whose story did you identify most strongly?

5. Did this book inspire you to read more about the history of Islam and Muslims?

6. Some writers insist that a "clash of civilizations" is inevitable. Others have claimed that a person cannot be both a faithful Muslim and a loyal American citizen. What do you think?

7. Do you adhere to a religion that has a sacred scripture? Do you know what every word in scripture means? Do you take every word literally? If not, why not?

8. Some of the authors in *I Speak for Myself* discuss juggling motherhood and career. How do their stories compare with yours?

9. What is there about the Muslim head covering that provokes such reflexive reactions in many non-Muslims? Is it different from nuns' habits? Jewish orthodox head coverings? What are the issues involved in religious dress?

10. What are the parameters of dress and modesty in our own world, religious or non-religious?

11. Are the words "objective," and "biased" appropriate to a discussion of religion? How are they used in the public discourse? Is there an objective view or only different points of view?

12. There has been a rise in attacks on Muslims and mosques in the United States. Has Islamophobia effected your community? How do you respond to Islamophobia?

13. What is the role of religion in politics? How does religion impact our public discourse on where we are going politically or culturally as a nation?

14. What would you like to investigate further after reading this book?

Acclaimed Books on Islam from White Cloud Press

Approaching the Qur'án: The Early Revelations
by Michael Sells
Paperback: $21.95 (includes audio files of Quranic recitations)

"Michael Sells has performed an invaluable service in making the beauty, spiritual energy, and compelling power of the Qur'an accessible to a Western audience for the first time."
—Karen Armstrong, author of *The Case for God* and *Muhammad: A Biography of the Prophet*

"The best version of Muslim scriptures available in English."
—Carl Ernst, professor of Islamic studies at the University of North Carolina and author of *The Shambhala Guide to Sufism*

The Muslim Next Door:
The Qur'án, The Media, and that Veil Thing
by Sumbul Ali-Karamali
Paperback: $16.95

"A beautiful book. At a time when most Americans are bombarded with misinformation about Islam and, in particular, about American Muslims, Ali-Karamali has written an elegant corrective. For anyone who truly wants to know what Muslims believe, this is the perfect book."
—Reza Aslan, author of *No god but God*

The Green Sea of Heaven:
Fifty ghazals from the Díwán of Háfiz
by Hafiz, translated by Elizabeth T. Gray, Jr.
Paperback: $14.95

"A translation…with a tender and poetic care that is both a scholarly and artistic joy."
—*The Harvard Review*

WHITE CLOUD PRESS
www.whitecloudpress.com   800-380-8286